RUSHDIE:

Haunted by His Unholy Ghosts

RUSHDIE:

Haunted by His Unholy Ghosts

By

Arshad Ahmedi

AVON BOOKS
1 DOVEDALE STUDIOS
465 BATTERSEA PARK ROAD
LONDON SW11 4LR

Printed and bound in the U.K.

Avon Books

London

First Published 1997

© Arshad Ahmedi, 1997

ISBN 1 86033 481 4

"The moving finger writes; and having writ,
Moves on; nor all your Piety nor Wit
Shall lure it back to cancel half a line,
Nor all your Tears wash out a word of it."

(From the 'Rubaiyat of Omar Khayyam' translated by Edward Fitzgerald).

ACKNOWLEDGEMENTS

My deepest gratitude goes to Hadhrat Mirza Tahir Ahmad, Khalifatul Masih IV, supreme head of the worldwide Ahmadiyya Muslim Community, who had confidence in me and assigned me this research project. His constant guidance throughout was the very much needed beacon which I looked up to and which gave me the strength and resolve to see it through to completion.

To Rizwan Mirza for his initial research.
To Mrs Shaukia Mir, Tanveer Khokhar and Safir Bhatti for their technical and professional assistance.
To the ever-smiling Waleed Ahmad for his extremely useful contributions.
To John Burke and the staff of Avon Books.
To Fareed Ahmad and Fazal Shahid Ahmad especially, who have both burnt the midnight oil on many an occasion in their quest to see the project to fruition, with their technical know-how and helpful suggestions. Fazal has proved conclusively, in my opinion, that there is indeed some life after Wimbledon Football Club!

FOREWORD

Almost the whole of the Western world was outraged at the pronouncement of the edict of the Fatwa, by Ayatollah Khomeini of Iran, on the author Salman Rushdie after the publication of *The Satanic Verses*. The entire issue was diverted from the deep insult and injury it caused to Muslims all over the world to a simplified matter of 'freedom of expression'. The Western media in particular had a field day in renewing its attacks on Islam and the whole fabric of Muslim society. All the latent fires of anti-Islam were rekindled, which have been instrumental in creating a bigger rift between Islam and the West.

In the aftermath of the grave episode of 'The Rushdie Affair' a lot of questions needed to be, and were, asked. Who was, or were, to blame for threatening the very real prospects of bringing the whole world together under the banner of peace? Does the right of freedom of 'expression' give one the license wilfully to injure the feelings of millions of fellow citizens? Is it permissible to cross deliberately the bounds of decency while hiding behind the guise of 'fiction'? Was Salman Rushdie really a Muslim? What was his knowledge of Islam, and what indeed are his true feelings towards Islam and how have they changed over the years? Was *The Satanic Verses* a religious controversy or was it a political time bomb right from the start?

Even after being forewarned that *The Satanic Verses* would become an item too hot to handle, how could a single man like Rushdie take on the whole of the Muslim world on his own and expect to get away with it?

What was it that clouded his decision to go ahead with its publication regardless?

Rushdie : Haunted by his Unholy Ghosts goes in depth to answer all these questions and much more, with relevant quotations from authentic sources. The book, in fact, starts at the very inception of Islam and traces the anti-Islamic conspiracy right through to the present day.

Contents

PART II

APPENDICES

INTRODUCTION

When Salman Rushdie published his so-called novel in 1988, it unleashed an unprecedented controversy throughout the world. Marches were organised and demonstrations were raised protesting against the contents of the book. In view of the depth of feeling that was aroused, some of these meetings inevitably broke into violence and several people were injured or killed.

As Muslim countries around the globe condemned the publication and the Ayatollah Khomeini of Iran issued his now infamous fatwa, Western nations went to the other extreme. They defended the publication to the hilt. This was typified by the reaction in Britain where the book was first published. Here, the British establishment claimed it could do nothing because it had to uphold the right of freedom of speech. By doing so, it had conveniently overlooked its own debacle in the 'Spy Catcher' affair and its subsequent and successful banning of satellite transmission of pornographic television channels into the UK. As far as the British establishment was concerned, it seems, transmission of abusive language on the airwaves could contravene its sacred tenet of freedom of speech but the publication of abusive language inflicted against the pure characters of revered individuals, causing hurt and anguish to hundreds of thousands of its citizens, could not.

Then, as if adding insult to injury, the book was heralded as a work of literature and was even nominated for the prestigious Booker Prize. The author was treated like a hero and extracts from his infamous book were read out in public.

i

When Muslims protested, they were branded as intolerant and medieval in their thinking. The burning of a copy of Salman Rushdie's book in public in the city of Bradford did not help matters, for it was promptly picked up by the media and shown repeatedly. This enraged the Western Muslim public even more and made an otherwise docile and law-abiding Muslim community living in peace for decades become militant and aggressive in its attitude.

Thus, when Muslims in Britain tried to seek redress in the courts, their efforts were doomed from the start. In a multi-religious society, British blasphemy laws, it appeared, only protected Christians from injury, and not the members of other faiths, certainly not Muslims.

Needless to say, with all this publicity, the book became a best seller overnight. Despite bans in numerous countries, it sold hundreds of thousands of copies in the first year and has become one of Viking's best sellers ever in history. Salman Rushdie's fate, however was sealed. Threats and feelings of animosity from the opponents of the book forced him into hiding and he was compelled to change his home 54 times in the space of the first two years. However, with it came notoriety, and he was portrayed as a symbol of freedom and free speech. The British Government poured thousands of pounds of taxpayers' money to fund his protection and he was given special audiences with the President of the United States, and the Prime Minister of Britain.

This contrast in their attitude towards Rushdie by the Muslims on the one hand and the West on the other mirrors the stark difference in their reaction. *Rushdie: Haunted by his Unholy Ghosts* charts a course that lies between the two. It rejects some of the extremism expressed by the East, but also condemns the attitude of the West. The issuing of the fatwa, it shows, cannot be substantiated by Islamic teachings. Nor can these condone some of the excesses committed in protesting against the book.

When condemning the attitude of the West, Arshad Ahmedi goes a step further in trying to reveal its sinister role in the whole affair. He demonstrates that the publication of such an injurious novel was not an isolated event but a product of hatred towards Islam and its

ii

founder that has been brewing up ever since its inception some 14 centuries ago. This is examined in detail from the intrigues that took place at the time of the Holy Prophet(sa) through to the barbarity of the Crusades, echoes of which were found in recent times during the Gulf War of 1991.

He also explores the role played by Western Orientalists who, giving an air of sincerity, always managed to sow the seeds of hatred against Islam and its founder in their writings. This history of animosity against Islam has been fuelled by some Muslims themselves. Dazzled by the material progress of the West, some 'intellectual Muslims' began to acquiesce to its view of Islam and share a distaste for it. Salman Rushdie is a product of this genre. The author has been examined in detail and an effort has been made to study all his writings. He has been noted to have a preoccupation if not a fetish for writing lewdly about sex and such passages invariably feature in his writings, including those for children.

Rushdie is also noted to be vain and conceited and someone who has been hankering after publicity. It was the prospect of being able to court such publicity that prompted him, at least in part, to write such a controversial novel. The book he eventually wrote attempted to assassinate the character of the Holy Prophet(sa) and other revered personalities in the history of Islam. But assassins seldom act alone and here Ahmedi reveals compelling evidence, circumstantial if nothing else, that other agencies must have been at play. How, he argues, could an author who himself has claimed not to have any interest in Islam, write abusive passages against its personalities and do so in such a way as to inflict the maximum injury to those who revere them? Why, he adds, was such a large sum paid to the author well before its printing and why did the publishers consistently refuse to refrain from going ahead with the publication despite advance warnings from some of its most prominent advisors? These questions and others can only be resolved if one concludes that Rushdie was put up to this and mischief was the ultimate purpose.

Such mischief may assuage one's feelings of hatred for Islam but it does little for race relations. Its impact has been considerable in Britain and a void has been driven between its Muslim public and the indigenous population. Extremist Muslim groups like Hizbe-Tahir and the Khalafah Movement have taken stronger root. Their antics have further strengthened the West's suspicion of Islam and engendered mistrust between the two communities. This cycle has to stop. The West needs to relinquish its view of Islam from the perspective of the Crusades and its age-old battles with the realm of Islam. It needs to abandon its policy of beating ordinary Muslims *into* fundamentalism and then beating them *for* fundamentalism.

But all is not doom and gloom. For amidst the voices condemning Islam, there are those in the West, like Prince Charles, who recognise this folly and are calling for a greater understanding. However, fostering greater understanding is a two way process. Arshad Ahmedi's work goes a long way to presenting an uncompromising but conciliatory Muslim response. By putting *The Satanic Verses* in its true context, it helps Muslims to deal with their wounded feelings in a measured and responsible manner. It attempts to build bridges without yielding an inch on matters of faith. By doing so, and by presenting the real image of Islam, it helps to allay some of the fears of the West and dampens its animosities towards those who hold this faith. It therefore has something positive to offer to people of all backgrounds, whether they are from the East or the West, Muslim or non-Muslim. As such, this book is invaluable and should prove to be an interesting read.

Waleed Ahmad, 1996

PART I

CHAPTER ONE

EARLY ATTACKS ON ISLAM AND THE HOLY PROPHET(SA)

The attacks on Islam, as with all religions, started at the very time of its inception. As soon as the Holy Prophet Muhammad (may peace and blessings of Allah be upon him) made the claim to prophethood, practically the whole of Mecca turned against him overnight. No stone was left unturned in the Meccans' evil and nefarious designs to put a quick end to this new faith, to this idea of the worship of just one God. The followers of Muhammad(sa) were meted out the severest punishments and the cruellest tortures ever inflicted upon any people in the history of mankind.

The early attacks on Islam were those of a physical nature; the thinking of its enemies being that a quick end to Muhammad(sa) would nip the new religion of Islam in the bud; and to do this the enemies were bent upon wiping it out by every available means. But true religions have a latent resilient quality, a feature that cannot be taken away by force. So with Islam.

These forceful attempts proved unsuccessful and with every passing day Islam spread with unprecedented success and, as history bears out, very soon the whole of Arabia had accepted Islam. Even

1

after the death of Muhammad(sa), Islam continued to gather momentum and before long it was knocking on Europe's door.

It was roughly at this time that the attacks on Islam took on a literary mode, headed by some Christian and Jewish writers who took it as their birthright and raison d'etre to try and find faults and inconsistencies in the Holy Qur'an and the Traditions of Hadith. They would use any means to attack Islam and to single out the Holy Prophet(sa) for the vilest of abuse.

This was perhaps how the Jews and Christians, who seem to have forgotten the struggles of their very own prophets, unwittingly came to be united in thought and action against their common enemy, Islam. The scenario is succinctly presented in the words of the Promised Messiah(as), Hadhrat Mirza Ghulam Ahmad, the founder of the Ahmadiyya Movement in Islam:

'Christians are out to destroy Islam and ready to use lies and fabrications in ways most subtle, and on all occasions and with the help of ever new techniques all directed to beguile and lead people astray. Christians are defaming and lampooning the Holy Prophet(sa), the perfect man who proved himself the pride of holy men of all times and chief among saints and apostles of the world. They hesitate not to caricature him in theatrical shows. They try and project a most hateful image they can invent of him. The worst that vicious and unchaste minds can think of is levelled against Islam and the Holy Prophet(sa) of Islam to lower them in the eyes of the world... The campaign is backed by the most complex fabrications and the most carefully planned devices that Christians can design. It is pursued mercilessly, with no thought of expenditure involved. It does not exclude some most shameful devices which decency forbids us to detail. It is a campaign let loose on a large scale and pushed by the worst possible wizardry by Christian peoples.'

(Victory of Islam, pp. 34)

Contemporary Western Orientalists have also admitted to the ulterior motives of their counterparts throughout the centuries. Maxime Rodinson, a French orientalist, in his book simply entitled *Mohammed*, admits to the motives of the Western writers though he excludes himself from this category. He openly denounces the Koran as the book of Allah, though he says that he respects the faith of the Muslims and adds:

> 'But I do not share it and I do not wish to fall back as many orientalists have done, on equivocal phrases to disguise my real meaning.'
>
> (Rodinson, *Mohammed* p. 218).

Hans Kung, another outspoken German theologian, also admits to the Christians' real motives for the study of the Qur'an, even as far back as the Middle Ages. He writes in *Christianity and the World Religions*:

> 'For his part, Luther had spoken out in favour of translating and publishing the Qur'an, but only so that everyone could see what an accursed, shameful, desperate book it was, full of lies, fabrications, and all sorts of horrors.'
>
> (Kung, *Christianity and the World Religions* p. 20).

Hans Kung has tried to give a schematised formula to describe the attitude of Western Christendom, over the centuries, toward Islam, as that which started 'from Ignorance through Arrogance to Tolerance'.

He is not too far off the mark but I think he is being rather generous in implying that scholars are more tolerant now. It may certainly be true of the general public, but the scholarly opinion is more determined than ever to maintain their distorted picture of Islam through their sheer hatred of the religion of Muhammad(sa). A more appropriate schematised formula that could apply to those scholars today would be 'from Ignorance through Arrogance to Abhorrence!

3

COMPARISON OF ATTACKS

A comparison can be drawn between the physical attacks on Islam in its very early years and the contemporary ones. During the time of the Holy Prophet(sa), especially in the various battles, the Muslims were always at a disadvantage. They were outclassed physically; they were fewer in numbers; they were poorly equipped; they had fewer camels and horses; and most of them were untrained in the art of warfare and on the field of battle.

The Meccans, however, were far greater in numbers (sometimes in the ratio of 3:1); they had much greater provisions, weapons, horses and camels; and above all, they were all well-trained and seasoned soldiers. But it was the Muslims who were awarded victories time and time again because they were in a different class spiritually and because of their unerring and unyielding belief in the one God and their total and sincere loyalty to their supreme leader. Moreover, the qualities they had in abundance were based totally on truth and honesty, and perseverance in the face of adversity.

If we compare that period of time with the present, we note the harsh similarity. Everything of advantage is at the disposal of the Judaeo-Christian nations of the West. Their total control of the media, radio, television and newspapers, though it is not always obvious, all employed ceaselessly in attacking Islam and all that it stands for, from every conceivable angle and without missing any opportunity, is like the Meccan superiority in weapons at that time.

Their physical strength is still ever-present, this was clearly visible in the recent Gulf War when their bully-boy browbeating tactics were employed, whereby the might of the Allies was pitted against one Muslim nation. The motives of the 'Allied' Western nations were all too plain to see but I do not intend to discuss this topic at length.

It is to the poisoned pens of the Western orientalists that I would like to respond and to expose those whose magic and wizardry have been employed to stimulate dangerous thoughts and satanic impulses.

Together with the orientalists are other philosophers and commentators (including some liberally reformed Muslims), who become so engrossed in these studies that they begin to lose their religious convictions. They begin to hold Divine Truths in contempt. The Being and Existence of God are not serious propositions with them. A great many are anti-religious, and being steeped in naturalistic thinking, they become hostile to religion.

College-going young men, even before they are out of college, say good-bye to their faith and their duties towards the faith. It was to this similar background that one such person entered the scene and became an ideal tool for the West to exploit, and, with a carrot of untold riches dangled in front of him, he became a more than willing accomplice. That person was Salman Rushdie. He would have done well to heed the advice of Hadhrat Mirza Ghulam Ahmad(as), the Promised Messiah and Mahdi, who wrote in one of his poems:

> Incline not, O brother!
> to the wealth of this wretched world.
> Deadly poison is every drop
> that seems like honey to you.

It was in fact the pen of Salman Rushdie that turned out to be the one with the deadliest poison of all when he wrote *The Satanic Verses*. How did this all come about? What made him do the impossible and think the unthinkable? Was there more to it than just the monetary guerdon? Was it apolitical or was it to do with religion? Or was it a conspiratory association of all these put together by the enemies of Islam? Was it then presented to Salman Rushdie as a full package, with advance royalties and with strings attached, and was he then told to go ahead and 'do your damnedest'? He must have felt like a child given the opportunity to run riot in a chocolate factory. He could have hardly believed his greedy eyes. But what the facts bear out is that he came out of it like an animal,

5

totally covered in filth and reeking of greed, hypocrisy, heresy, blasphemy and apostasy!

THE SHADOWS BEHIND RUSHDIE

Rushdie must have known the consequences. Surely, he could not have been that naive - or were the powers and forces behind him too great to resist and too powerful to desist? Or, to coin a dramatic phrase in true Mafiosi style, was he made an offer he could not refuse? There can be no denying that this was not the work of Salman Rushdie alone. His very limited knowledge of Islam coupled with a totally un-Islamic upbringing, the huge financial backing to this project and the similarity with earlier literary attacks on the Holy Prophet(sa) and Islam, all point to a powerful conspiracy against the religion that is regarded as a threat to Western thinking and idealism.

All the signs point to a conspiracy between the Jews and the Christians in collusion with a mercenary, or indeed a modern day Faust. It was as if this union or marriage was devised and made, not in Heaven, but in the other place!

I shall examine just some of the attacks on Islam and the Holy Prophet(sa) from medieval times to the present day, which show harsh similarities, through the literary works of commentators and orientalists. It will become evident how the same limited school of thought and references has been employed by the Western writers throughout the centuries and how they have tried to portray a completely distorted and untenable image of Islam and of its Prophet(sa). It will also become evident that the finished package of *The Satanic Verses* is a culmination of all the previous attacks on the Holy Prophet(sa); the only difference being that this book was presented in a most vindictive and malicious fashion using the foulest of language.

6

CHAPTER TWO

THE CRUSADES

To trace the shadows behind the evil thinking of *The Satanic Verses*, we have to go back in time; right back in fact to the time of the medieval attacks on Islam by the Christian Crusaders which instigated the first of the real and serious Muslim - Christian encounters.

Muslims had begun to make territorial progress throughout Europe and it is true to say that the 'Europeans had felt great admiration for the superior state of Arab culture, philosophy, science, and medicine, as well as for the economic and military power of Islam.' (Hans Kung, *Christianity and the World Religions*, p. 20).

Many Christians, including their rulers, began to adopt the customs of the Muslims and many started to convert to Islam. Western historians have called this the period of Islamic Colonialism! No matter what they may choose to call it, the fact remains that this was a period in history that even the Western writers refer to as one of religious tolerance whereby the Christians and Jews had the option of becoming protected minorities and were able to live in peace and without fear, and freely practice their faith. Hans Kung admits to the tolerance of Muslims and makes a striking comparison with the Christians:

'In the medieval Islamic world, Christians and Jews could actually practice their religions more freely than in many present-day totalitarian states. And the contrast with the Christian Middle Ages is striking. Pogroms were relatively rare, and Muslims could scarcely feel within their rights taking part in them: They were not only morally reprehensible, but violations of the law; and since the law was divine, they were also a sin.'

(op cit., p. 104).

As with all great powers in history, a time comes when cracks begin to appear and, slowly, but surely, the seemingly impossible happens and the power of a once great empire transfers from one hand to another. And this is what happened to the Muslim rule in the West at the turn of the 11th Century, which was directly in keeping with the Divine Plan as prophecied in the Holy Qur'an.

A process of disintegration began in the 11th century and there was a break-up of Muslim rule which gave an opportunity to the Christian princes in north-west Spain, (hitherto semi-independent and paying tribute to the central Muslim government) to make themselves fully independent and to extend the territories that they controlled.

Gradually, Muslim power was transferred from the Almoravids and the Berbers to the Almohads. After the disappearance of the Almohads, the Christian Reconquista made rapid progress. Although even the Spanish historians are divided about the interpretation of the Reconquista, what is quite evident is that it was initiated to stem the tide of Islamic culture and thinking which was about to sink that of the Christians. So advanced was the Islamic culture that the Christians were unable to rationalise why they had to remove the Muslims from Spain. Even as late as 1602, the Archbishop of Valencia, when providing Philip III with reasons for driving out the Muslims, commented that:

'they commended nothing so much as that liberty of conscience, in all matters of religion, which the Turks and all other Muhammadans suffer their subjects to enjoy.'

The poor Christians were forced to worship in freedom, celebrate openly, and the dastardly Muslims even helped them to build churches!

Another historian, Hugh Trevor-Roper, in *The Rise of Christian Europe* has commented on the dubious motives of the Crusades which went hand in hand with other forms of European advance and had nothing to do with the rescue of the Holy Places :

'...the advance of Spanish Christians against the Moors of Spain, the advance of German settlers against the Slavs in eastern Europe, the conquest of Ireland by the Anglo-Norman barons of England, the conquest of Languedoc by the barons of northern France, and the conquest of Byzantium itself, and all its empire, by Frankish barons.......we realise that those two centuries were centuries of a general European expansion, and that the Crusades, whether we like them or not, were an inseparable part of that expansion.'

(p. 29)

The Crusades had for a long time been regarded by Western historians as a combined spiritual and material counter-attack of the enslaved West against its Muslim exploiters, and the struggle had been sensationalised as that between East and West, or between Christendom and Islam. Some have even labelled the Crusading movement as a Christian Jihad against the Muslims!

It has been recorded in history that the true and real motives of the Christian Crusaders had been to rescue their Holy places and to save Christianity from being swamped by the infidels. But what their ideals were and how they achieved them are two completely different things. I shall quote passages from the Western writers themselves who admit to the un-Christian-like behaviour of the European Christians during the Crusades.

David Hume, an 18th Century historian, saw the Crusades as a 'universal frenzy, an epidemic fury of fanatical and romantic warriors, the most durable monument of human folly that has yet appeared in any age or nation.' (op cit., p. 28). Leonard W. Levy, Professor of Humanities at the Claremont Colleges in USA, in his widely-acclaimed and controversial book, *Treason Against God* also

9

talks of the age of the Crusades as incredibly savage:

'The Crusaders indiscriminately massacred Moslems and Jews in the Holy Land, not sparing women and children.'

(pp. 115/116).

What was to be a Holy War turned out in the end to be barbarism on a grand scale. But the Christian writers of that age and subsequent centuries upheld the actions of the marauding Crusaders and justified their every savage act and painted the saviours of Christianity in glory and martyrdom. Hugh Trevor-Roper, a British historian, relates some of these in his book and quotes Edward Gibbon:

'The simple Crusaders, who paused to chronicle their violent but holy deeds, and ended each chapter of carnage with devout scriptural ejaculations, questioned their own motives no more than the Spanish conquistadors of the sixteenth century. To them, the Turks were the infamous, accursed unbelievers, God's enemies and ours, while the Christians who perished in battle went up to Heaven to be robed in white and receive the palm of martyrdom.'

(*The Rise of Christian Europe*, p. 101).

Trevor-Roper also relates some of the views of the fashionable Jesuit Louis Maimbourg, who also upheld the actions of the Crusaders:

'To him the Crusades were still holy wars, whose every barbarity was justified by their high spiritual aim; and he described with relish how the Christians, once in possession of Jerusalem, used to their full extent the rights of victory...... Everywhere one could see nothing but heads flying, legs hacked off, arms cut down, bodies in slices....they killed the very children in their mothers arms to exterminate, if possible, that accursed race, as God formerly wished should be done to the Amalekites.'

(p. 101-102).

10

Sir Steven Runciman tries to give a balanced contemporary Christian view of the Crusades at the conclusion of his three-volume *A History of the Crusades*. Though the language and tone has been softened, the brutality and savagery of the crusaders is still borne out:

'The triumphs of the Crusade were the triumphs of faith. But faith without wisdom is a dangerous thing......the Crusades were a tragic and destructive episode. The historian as he gazes back across the centuries at their gallant story must find his admiration overcast by sorrow at the witness that it bears to the limitations of human nature. There was so much courage and so little honour, so much devotion and so little understanding. High ideals were besmirched by cruelty and greed, enterprise and endurance by a blind and narrow self-righteousness; and the Holy War itself was nothing more than a long act of intolerance in the name of God, which is the sin against the Holy Spirit.'
(*A History of the Crusades*; Harmondsworth: Penguin 1965; pp. 480)

CRUSADES, COLONIALISM AND IMPERIALISM

Even after the Christian nations of the West had driven the Muslims out of Europe, the British and the French began to invade their lands, during the 19th century . For example, in 1830 the French colonised Algiers, and in 1839 the British colonised Aden; between them they took over Tunisia (1881), Egypt (1882), the Sudan (1898) and Libya and Morocco (1912). In 1920, even though they had made pledges to the Arab countries that they would have their independence after the defeat of the Turkish Empire, Britain and France carved up the Middle East between them into mandates and protectorates. There has been a lot of debate and controversy over the association of the Crusades with European Colonialism and Christian missionary work; the West has been reluctant to accept this view, but some orientalists and Western writers have been honest enough to concede on this point. For example, Montgomery Watt in *Muslim-Christian Encounters* writes:

'The historically minded Christian today is not proud of the Crusades, and might allow that there was an element of colonialism in them.'

(p. 82).

Karen Armstrong, an English writer and broadcaster and a former Roman Catholic nun, is more forthright and sides with the popular Muslim view in her book *Muhammad, A Western Attempt To Understand Islam*:

'Today the Muslim world associates Western imperialism and Christian missionary work with the Crusades. They are not wrong to do so. When General Allenby arrived in Jerusalem in 1917, he announced that the Crusades had been completed, and when the French arrived in Damascus their Commander marched up to Saladin's tomb in the Great Mosque and cried: *Nous revenons, Saladin!* [We have returned, Saladin!] The Christian missionary effort supported the colonialists, attempting to undermine traditional Muslim culture in the conquered countries..... The colonialists would have argued that they were bringing progress and enlightenment, but the effort was informed with violence and contempt.'

(p. 40).

The brutality and savagery continued well into the 19th and 20th centuries. The pacification of Algeria, for example, took many years and any resistance was brutally put down in reprisal raids. The contemporary French historian M. Baudricourt gives us an idea of what one of those raids was like:

'Our soldiers returning from the expedition were themselves ashamed.....about 18,000 trees had been burnt; women, children and old men had been killed. The unfortunate women particularly excited cupidity by the habit of wearing silver ear-rings, leg-rings and arm-rings. These rings have no catch like French bracelets. Fastened in youth to the limbs of girls they cannot be removed when they are grown up. To get them off our soldiers

12

used to cut them off their limbs and leave them alive in a mutilated condition.'
(La Guerre et le gouvernement de l'Algerie, Paris, 1853, p. 160).

ISLAMIC COMPARISON

In sharp contrast, how different were the conquests of the Muslims. Nowhere were any barbaric acts of carnage or brutality reported when Muslims won battles. How different were the humane teachings of the Holy Qur'an in the treatment of prisoners of war, and the teachings regarding the behaviour of the victors over the vanquished. And this has never been displayed any better than by the example of Muhammad(sa).

The entry into Mecca of the victorious Muslims, with the Holy Prophet(sa) of Islam at the head, was an event that has been unsurpassed in history in terms of benificence and forgiveness. The thoughts of the Holy Prophet(sa) and his Companions must have gone back to the years and years of persecution that they had suffered at the hands of the Meccans; they had been tortured beyond the boundaries of humanity; they had seen their families and loved ones butchered and massacred just because they professed belief in one God.

And now finally, when they stood victorious with the enemy literally at their feet, what would their reaction be? Muhammad Zafrulla Khan, a distinguished Ahmadi scholar in world religions, sets the scene beautifully in his book, *Muhammad, Seal of The Prophets*:

'The Holy Prophet (sa), peace be on him, sent for the leaders of Quraish and asked them how he should deal with them. They replied that they fully merited whatever punishment he might choose to inflict upon them, but that they knew he was a generous brother and would deal with them as such. The Holy Prophet (sa) pronounced judgement in the words addressed by Joseph to his brethren: No retribution shall be exacted from you this day (Ch. 12, v. 93). He told them they were free. All the scorn

13

and ridicule poured on him by the Meccans; their implacable hatred and enmity; the long years of bitter, cruel and sustained persecution; all the fighting, the hardship and suffering; the loss of dear and devoted Companions, all - all was in the moment of triumph laid aside, banished from the mind and forgiven in the name of the Lord On High, the Gracious, the Merciful, the Creator and Master of all........

The gates of love and mercy were opened wide. Bitter enemies of the morning became warm friends by midday. Some hearts were still sullen; the humiliation, though softened by magnanimity, was hard to endure, but even these could not long withstand the healing effect of the balm so generously and beneficently applied by the Prophet of God. History furnishes no parallel instance of such complete forgiveness, such utter beneficence, on so large a scale.'

(Zafrullah Khan, *'Muhammad - Seal of The Prophets'* pp. 235-236).

This beneficence and generosity was later displayed by the Khalifas of Islam and subsequent leaders, like the legendary Saladin, who has been given the highest of praises even by the Western historians. The great French writer, Voltaire, named Saladin as one of his heroes:

'The great enemy of the crusaders, Saladin, who having beaten the Christians in battle, bequeathed his wealth impartially to the Moslem, Jewish and Christian poor.'

(*The Rise of Christian Europe*, p 104).

The romantic novelist Sir Walter Scott also admired the virtues of Saladin which he associated with those of a noble European sovereign, and at the same time was also aware of the cruelty and violence of his hero, Richard the Lionheart. In his introduction to his tale of the Crusades, *The Talisman*, he writes:

'The period relating more immediately to the Crusades...was that at which the warlike character of Richard I, wild and generous, a pattern of chivalry, with all its extravagant virtues, and its no less absurd errors, was opposed to that of Saladin, in which the Christian and English monarch showed all the cruelty

14

and violence (supposed to characterise an Eastern ruler); and Saladin on the other hand, displayed the deep policy and prudence of a European sovereign.'

(M-C Encounters, pp. 79/80).

The same contrasting behaviour is seen in Spain where the coming of Islam completely transformed Spain from a living hell to a paradise on earth, and this is summed up in the words of the writer Stanley Lane-Poole:

> '...Never was Andalusia so mildly, justly, and wisely governed as by her Arab conquerors....the people were on the whole contented - as contented as any people can be whose rulers are of a separate race and creed, - and far better pleased than they had been when their sovereigns belonged to the same religion as that which they nominally professed...'

(The Moors in Spain)

The Muslims allowed the conquered people freedom to follow their religious faith whatever it might be. (Albert & E Vail - *Transforming Light*). The manner in which the Muslims governed this mixture of peoples and faith is explained by Stanley Lane-Poole as follows:

> 'The subject peoples 'were permitted to retain their own laws and judges; ...they had even gained the right which had never been permitted them by Gothic kings; they could alienate their lands. In religious toleration they had nothing to regret. Instead of persecuting them and forcing upon them a compulsory conversion, as the Goths had upon the Jews, the Arabs left them free to worship whom or what they pleased. ...the best proof of the satisfaction of the Christians with their new rules is the fact that there was not a single religious revolt during the eighth century.'

In Rodney Castleden's *World History* (Paragon 1994) there is mention after mention of the sufferings of the Jewish subjects at the hands of other races but not a single reference to their wanton large-scale persecution by the Muslims.

The truth of the matter is that the Muslims have always displayed noble characteristics but the majority of the Christian writers have never had the fair-play attitude to extol the virtues of their adversaries. The method that they had employed to immunise Christians against competing belief systems like Islam was to slander the competition by any means.

CHAPTER THREE

HATRED FOR ISLAM

It is quite obvious that the West fully realises the brutality and the shamefulness of the Crusades, and with so many writers and historians relating the infamous episodes and condemning them, it would seem that they would have learnt something from them. Far from it! The irony is that despite being tainted with these dishonourable facts of history, the Christian nations in power today still display the same acts of savagery and brutality.

In the recent Gulf War for example, they all ganged up against one nation. The Allied Powers humbled Iraq within a matter of weeks, with their heavy aerial bombardment, killing indiscriminately anyone that happened to be in their line of fire, including innocent civilians, women and children. All this was done in the so-called name of Justice. The modern-day crusaders justified this by putting a veil around their brutal actions and disguised them as those of virtue and nobility.

Because the Gulf War was initially between two Muslim countries, the Christian powers were not concerned as to which nation they should side with as long as it meant the destruction of at least one of them. Such is still the hatred for Islam!

Even in the present Bosnian War, the West had superficially shown concern for the wronged Bosnian Muslims and if the West had really wanted to put an end to the hostilities and atrocities being

17

perpetrated against the Bosnian Muslims, then they could have settled the war in weeks just as they did in the Gulf War, due to the massive strength of the combined Allies. But the war was allowed to continue for almost four years and things were getting progressively worse rather than better in that time. This is a classic example of the two-faced bigotry of the West, and the United Nations has been shown up yet again for its ineffectiveness and worthlessness.

The hatred for Islam by the West is all too plain and all too clear to see. Only the world does not wish to observe and turns a blind eye to the hell being presented right in front of them.

For some reason the Christian nations of the West display a vampirish concupiscence for the blood of Islam - the blood of no other faith or religion seems as satiating to them as that of Islam.

There seems to be no fear of other world religions like Buddhism or Hinduism. Is it because Islam does not enjoy the aura of transfiguring distance and exotic magic that surrounds the image of these Indian religions in the mind of the general public? Professor Josef van Ess, a German historian, expresses his views on this subject of the hatred for Islam in Hans Kung's *Christianity and the World Religions*:

'Interest in Islam goes way back .....The things one hears or reads in the media about Islam, like the things intellectuals generally have to say about it are alarming. Alarming in a double sense: first, because of the bias and prejudices that these judgements betray, and second because of the demonising accent with which they are rendered. Nobody is afraid of Buddhism or Hinduism; vis-à-vis Islam, however, fear is the normal attitude... In this sort of climate, stereotypes flourish; the desire for information is all too quickly satisfied by generalisations and hasty conclusions.... anti-Islamic clichés lie deep in the sub-conscious and often meet with unanimous approval, for example in newspaper cartoons. This is because Islam doesn't form part of our cultural heritage.... Teachers were and still are hardly

18

prepared to handle the subject.'

(Kung, *Christianity and the World Religions*, pp. 5-6).

Hans Kung, in the same book, expresses a similar fear:

'Over the course of history, Islam has often been a disturbing, threatening, alarming reality for Christendom; and in fact for most Christians it still remains almost two thousand years after Christ and fourteen hundred years after Muhammad a sinister phenomenon, despite (and because of) our geographical nearness to it. With the finger on the pulse of contemporary life, recently popular writers have treated the resurgence of Islam once again as an ominous turning point in the history of the West. Let's admit the fact: Islam continues to strike us as essentially foreign, as more threatening, politically and economically, than either Hinduism or Buddhism, a phenomenon, in any case, that we have a hard time understanding.'

(p. 19).

Karen Armstrong, a contemporary English writer, talks of the attempt by Jewish and Christian scholars to reach a new understanding 'after centuries of virulent Christian anti-Semitism'. Why are the scholars of these two great religions, Judaism and Christianity, suddenly willing to make amends for past hostilities?

Perhaps they are putting aside their differences to work together to stem the tide of 'The Great Enemy,' Islam, from running havoc in the West.

Islam is certainly regarded as the outsider as far as the goodwill of the whole world is concerned. Karen Armstrong is astute enough to admit this when she talks about Islam as being the one major religion which 'seems to be outside this circle of goodwill and, in the West at least, to have retained its negative image... even though it is the third religion of Abraham and more in tune with our own Judaeo-Christian tradition... But the old hatred of Islam continues to flourish on both sides of the Atlantic and people have few scruples about attacking this religion, even if they know little about it.'

19

Armstrong goes on to explain the reason for this hatred:

'The hostility is understandable, because until the rise of the Soviet Union in our own century, no polity or ideology posed such a continuous challenge to the West as Islam. When the Muslim empire was established in the seventh century CE, Europe was a backward region. Islam had quickly overrun much of the Christian world of the Middle East as well as the great Church of North Africa... This brilliant success was threatening; had God deserted the Christians and bestowed his favour on the infidel? Even when Europe recovered from the Dark Ages and established its own great civilisation, the old fear of the ever-expanding Muslim empire remained. Europe could make no impression on this powerful and dynamic culture..... This fear made it impossible for Western Christians to be rational or objective about the Muslim faith.... Western scholars denounced Islam as a blasphemous faith and its Prophet Muhammad as the Great Pretender, who had founded a violent religion of the sword in order to conquer the world. Mahomet became a bogy to the people of Europe, used by mothers to frighten disobedient children.... This inaccurate image of Islam became one of the received ideas of Europe and it continues to affect our perceptions of the Muslim world.
(Armstrong, Muhammad, *A Western Attempt To Understand Islam*, pp. 10/11).

Most of what has been written about Islam, the Holy Prophet(sa) and other noble personages by the Western writers has been depreciative and disparaging, and that has been one of the reasons why the general public and the masses have been so mis-informed about Islam. Montgomery Watt is honest enough to admit that the good and salient points of Islam have not been projected enough to alter its distorted image:

'Many Christians came to appreciate the knightly generosity of a Saladin, but only a small amount of scholarly work was done. It was the scholars of France and Western Europe who created the new and more detailed image of Islam.'

(M-C Encounters, pp. 80/81).

And this 'new and more detailed image of Islam' was, in fact, presented in a most twisted and distorted fashion to negate all the virtues of Islam. I shall look at just some of the writers starting from the early period in medieval Europe.

CHAPTER FOUR

LITERARY ATTACKS ON ISLAM

The noteworthy attacks on Islam by Christian scholars started in medieval Europe, especially through the writings of the Byzantine theologians from 8th to the 13th centuries. These have been studied by Adel-Theodore Khoury, a Christian Arab who is professor at the University of Munster in Germany. The book is entitled *Polemique Byzantine Contre L'Islam* [Byzantine Polemics Against Islam] (VIIIe-XIIIeS) Leiden:Brill, 1972, pp. 359-365.

In these writings Islam is portrayed as a false religion tending towards idolatry. Muhammad(sa) is depicted as a false prophet, an emissary of the devil, inspired by the 'father of lies', and is indeed himself the Anti-Christ. Much is made, too, of what are held to be his moral lapses. The Qur'an is regarded as a false scripture, in which Muhammad(sa) not only included true material from the Old and New Testaments, but also added other material from heretics, such as Manichaeans, and inventions of his own. Islam was thus portrayed as a harmful religion of diabolic inspiration, and the Christian theologians would dearly have loved to bring about its destruction.

The defamatory and calumnious work was carried further by other scholars like Peter the Venerable, Ricoldo da Monte Croce and especially Thomas Aquinas. They produced books like *Disputations against the Saracens and the Qur'an*, which dealt with

22

Islam, and although some of the material was true and sound, they still managed to portray an image of Islam which was fourfold:

1. Islam is false and a deliberate perversion of truth, asserting that Muhammad mixed truth with falsehood.
2. Islam is a religion which spreads by force and violence and by the sword.
3. Islam is a religion of self-indulgence. In the perception of the daily life of Muslims sexuality was thought to play a great part. It was supposed that a Muslim could have many wives, not just four, but seven, or ten, or even more, and that in Paradise he was promised delectable female companions. One writer even thought that there was a verse in the Qur'an which permitted fornication, and other verses were imagined to permit or encourage abnormal sexual practices.
4. Muhammad is the Anti-Christ. Muhammad was regarded as a false prophet and as he was not really a prophet, he had established a religion in opposition to the religion of Christianity, so he must have been doing something evil, and he must, therefore, be a tool or agent of the Devil. In other words, he was the Anti-Christ.

The character of Muhammad(sa) was further maligned and traduced by alleging moral failures on his part; the main points being that Muhammad(sa) was insincere, sensual and treacherous. Thomas Carlyle vigorously used the attacks over a hundred years ago. These very important aspects of the distorted image of Islam, which was formed by Christian scholars in the 12th and 13th centuries, still tend to control European thinking to this day. For example, Maxime Rodinson, the famous French orientalist, in his book, *Mohammed* writes on the subject:

'For the Christians in particular, he became the arch-enemy, an object of execration, an epileptic fraud. The accounts given

23

of him by his disciples were taken and twisted to make a hideous portrait of a cruel and lascivious individual, steeped in every kind of viciousness and crime.'

(pp. 301/302).

Any rational thinking person will find this hard to believe.

COLONIALISM AND CHRISTIANITY

Over a period of three to four centuries, the Europeans, mainly the Portuguese, the British, the French and the Dutch, began to assert their power over the Asian and African continents at first through trade, and then gradually through political assertion and finally, through economic colonialism. Going hand-in-hand with these changes was the pressure applied by their missionaries who imposed Christianity on the indigenous people.

The European colonisation proved extremely unpleasant for the subjects and the rulers openly displayed an attitude of superiority over them. The Western historians readily admit to this. An example is in the speeches and writings of A.J. Balfour and Lord Cromer around 1910 dealing with British control of Egypt. They assumed British superiority without question and spoke of the 'oriental' as having all sorts of weaknesses: incapacity for self-government, social and moral degradation; inability to think logically, and so forth.

The colonialists certainly treated their subjects with less compassion than would be expected from a people whose religion advocates respect for human dignity. It is true that the Europeans were superior materially, and that the rest of the world benefited from their superior education and governing systems, but the sad part has been that they confused this type of superiority with moral superiority and this led them to regard the oriental and the African as a morally inferior being who was badly in need of guidance to the true light through Christianity. But even this was up to a certain point, and not beyond. Thomas Merton honestly analyses the relationship between white colonial administrators and the subjects that they ruled over in an article entitled 'Cargo Cults of the South

24

Pacific' in his book *Love and Living* (New York: Bantam Books 1980; p 77) :

'...of course we are willing to help our black brother, but the help is offered in arrogant, vain, self-complacent terms. We will only help him to be exactly like us, while at the same time making it impossible for him to be like us. So we put him in an impossible bind and then wonder why he feels anguished..... of course, we pretend we want to share our secret with everybody. We want to bring everybody else into the same affluence that we have. But we do not mean what we say. We want to use our inferiors for our own profit. We invest in them in such a way that the under-developed countries are maintained in subjection to us.'

This arrogance of the West which had almost reached its zenith as far as material power was concerned was foretold in the Holy Qur'an over 1400 years ago by God Almighty in Surat Al-Kahf, Chapter 18, verses 35-36, in which He gives a parable concerning the conditions of the two major peoples, Christians and Muslims:

"And he had fruit in abundance. And he said to his companion boastfully, arguing with him, I am richer than thou in wealth and strongest in respect of men. And he entered his Garden while he was wronging his soul. He said, I do not think that this will ever perish."

The above verses denote that, in their chequered history, Christian nations would rise to great power again and this began with the dawn of the 17th century AD when the Christian nations of Europe began to make great progress and acquire unprecedented power and prestige which reached its peak in the 19th century.

Being proud of their material progress, Western Christian nations would give themselves up to a life of ease and luxury and in their conceit and arrogance misconceive that their power, progress and prosperity will last for ever, and being lulled into a false sense of security and complacency, they would be entirely lost in a life of sin and iniquity.

And how this is proving to be true to the letter!

SUPERIOR WESTERN CULTURE?

Going back to the subjection of the people of the colonies, the temptation had always been placed in front of the subjects to taste the fruits of the supposedly superior Western culture, education and general way of life, but at the same time keeping the subjects at arm's length, always keeping them coming back for more, but never letting them take their fill.

The Western-type education provided was something that most of the local people wanted, and this included a lot of Muslims, but there was always pressure for the acceptance of Christianity. Even in the field of medicine, whereby hospitals and medical clinics were set up, there are reports of places where it was made a condition of treatment that the patients should attend services or listen to sermons.

A large number from the Hindus in India and from the primitive peoples in Africa succumbed to the material necessities and were converted to Christianity; there were, however, much fewer converts from Islam; perhaps due to the fact that at about the same time there were a lot of books published by Western scholars who had continued to present Islam in a distorted fashion and as there was a fundamentalist move back to Islam anyway, it seemed to have an adverse effect on the aims of the Christian missionaries.

So Islam has always proved to be the stumbling block for the Christian nations of the West. It has always been regarded as a threat to their plans of total world domination and they spared no expense to achieve their aims fully.

The hatred for Islam was evident in India as well. During the reign of the British it became abundantly clear that the rulers had greater affinity with the Hindus than the Muslims whom they despised. The obvious example is that of Earl Mountbatten, the last

26

Viceroy of India. In a recent programme on British television on Channel 4, entitled Secret Lives, and shown on 9 March 1995, a number of historians and biographers openly talked of Mountbatten's favouritism for the Hindu leader Nehru and his hatred for Muhammad Ali Jinnah, the founder of the Muslim state of Pakistan. The historians also blamed Mountbatten for inciting the civil war between Hindus and Muslims which claimed almost a million lives, most of them Muslims. On his return to England after India's independence, he received a hero's welcome from everyone, including the ruling Labour government headed by Attlee and all the Conservatives, congratulating him on his success in India.

Can the incitement of a civil war that claimed the lives of nearly a million people be regarded as an act of heroism?

But as destiny would have it, is it not incredibly ironic that almost thirty years after the massacre of a million people, Earl Mountbatten himself would be blown up into a million pieces as a target of an IRA bomb, which can only be described as a result of a civil war between two sects of a religion that is predominant in the West, Protestant and Roman Catholic Christians?

MUSLIM LIBERAL THOUGHT

At about the same time that the Fundamentalist movement back to Islam started, and the access to Western education and the negative appreciation of Islam by the Western orientalists was getting under way, it gave rise to liberal thought in the minds of some of the Muslim scholars. This was fully exploited by the orientalists who have attempted to suggest that the morals and ethics of Muslims somewhat deteriorated due to the strict and orthodox rules of Islam, and in order to be accepted as part of the Western society they had to forego some of the stricter habits and they had to relax their conservative attitude to religion.

From the middle of the last century to the present, there has certainly been a reconstruction of Muslim thought. There have been conservative reformers whose main concern has been to purify Islam

27

of all un-Islamic practices which had crept into it, by returning to the Qur'an and primitive traditions, whereas the liberal reformers realised that the purification of the House of Islam must go hand-in-hand with its modernisation. There have been some leading liberal scholars of the 19th and 20th centuries, notably Jamaluddin Afghani (1839-97), Muhammad Abduh (1849-1905) and Sir Syed Ahmad Khan (1817-98), who influenced the thinking of many an Indian Muslim. The British East India Company was a powerful body in India and was greatly influential in imposing its colonial imperialism and had great influence on the local indigenous population which included Hindus, Muslims and Christians.

As time went by, people slowly became torn between their loyalty to the British and their native patriotism. Many, including Indian Muslims, decided to declare their loyalty to the British and moreover, decided that their salvation lay only in the acquisition of Western learning. With these two aims in mind, they became convinced that British rule was better than the rule of the supposedly decadent Mughals, and also that if they wanted to prosper under it they had better start acquiring European science and learning.

There were those who foolishly and naively thought that the British Christians, rather than being out to destroy Islam, were its well-wishers and wanted the Muslims to develop socially, politically and economically. But they had not accounted for one major hazard which would retard this progress, or, in fact, stop it in its tracks from the very beginning.

The greatest obstacle to the material, social and intellectual progress of the Muslims was their conservative attitude to religion. The liberal reformers, in order to overcome this problem, saw the need to re-examine the foundations of the Islamic faith and advocated laxity in certain aspects to accommodate their secular ambitions.

And as is human nature, when laxity or any form of slackness appears, and you start to divert from the original teachings and you start becoming apologetic for what you believe in, and you begin to compromise, then the path that leads people astray knows no bounds, and slowly but surely it takes a progressively downward plunge.

A younger contemporary of Sir Syed Khan, the famous Indian modernist Ameer Ali Syed, published a book in 1873 called *The Spirit Of Islam*, which became the manifesto of Islamic liberalism. A considerable portion of the book is an apologia for certain actions of the Prophet which are often criticised by non-Muslim scholars.

Ameer Ali was yet another victim of the powerful influence of the Western orientalists' autocratic spell, and it was these types of liberal thinkers who regarded the pure monotheism and alleged rigid austerity of Islam as counter-productive to being accepted into the European way of life, and it was these types of liberals who tried to make aware wrongfully that many Islamic laws were outmoded and were inappropriate for the modern world. They wanted to prescribe the spirit and not the letter of the Islamic law. According to Ameer Ali, the spirit of the law is a love of righteousness, a striving after good works, a practice of the love of God and of His creatures. He quotes a tradition from Tirmidhi to show that the Prophet(sa) did not expect his law to be immutable but that he expected it to be observed less and less as men grew in true spirituality. And also according to Ameer Ali, many of Muhammad's laws were the result of temporary circumstances. As the circumstances ceased to exist, so the laws ceased to exist also!

What incredible ideas and thoughts had crept into the minds of so-called Muslims - the new breed of liberals who had tried to reconstruct the Muslim thought and who were playing right into the hands of the Christian orientalists.

It was this type of liberal thinking, in the middle of the19th century, that brought untold damage to, and rocked the very foundation of, Islam. Coupled with it was the Western orientalists' brutal and vicious attacks on the Holy Prophet(sa) of Islam, which continued to go unchecked and unabated. It wasn't any wonder then that Muslims in India began to find it increasingly difficult to practice their faith, thereby fulfilling another of the prophecies of the Holy Prophet(sa) that there would come a time when there would be nothing left of Islam but its name. In fact, many Muslims converted to Christianity, Hinduism and even Atheism. So much for the liberal thinking that the British should not be molested because they did not want to destroy Islam, but rather were its well-wishers and wanted the Muslims to succeed!!

How true again was the Word of God revealed 14 centuries ago, when He warned that the Jews and Christians will seek to extinguish the light of Allah, i.e. Islam. In Surat Al-Taubah, Chapter 9, verse 32:

'They (the Jews and Christians) seek to extinguish the light of Allah with their mouths; but Allah refuses but to perfect His light, though the disbelievers may resent it.'

The opponents of Islam must have been very pleased to see the religion of Muhammad(sa) in this sorry state, towards the end of the 19th century and being attacked on all sides by Hindus, Christians, Aryas and Atheists alike. Muslims were beginning to feel almost ashamed of their faith and began to give feeble excuses and apologies for their beliefs.

CHAPTER FIVE

THE APPEARANCE OF THE REFORMER OF THE AGE

Islam was certainly at an all-time-low. It was high time for the Reformer of the Age to appear and to make the claim to be the protector of the Faith and to restore Islam to its original purity and pristine quality!

This would fulfil yet another prophecy of the Holy Prophet(sa) of Islam. It was the plan of the Almighty that in the same way that Muhammad(sa) appeared amongst the people living in the darkest period of the Dark Ages, that of the period of Jahliyya (period of ignorance) when mankind was almost entirely bereft of spiritual light, so in the same way the Reformer of the Age would appear amongst the people who had all but obliterated the name of Islam from the face of the earth. And in the same way that Muhammad(sa) was 'the man of the hour', so similarly was the Reformer equipped to defend the faith of Islam.

The Reformer of the Age, Hadhrat Mirza Ghulam Ahmad(as), who made the claim to be the Promised Messiah and Mahdi that everyone had been waiting for, was the founder of the Ahmadiyya Movement in Islam. He defended Islam to the hilt using cogent, effective and convincing arguments to prove its truth; and he completely vindicated the name of Muhammad(sa) from the insults and the tarnished and tainted image portrayed of his noble character that was purity personified.

The Promised Messiah(as) also did something that none of the other Muslims had been able to do and that was to rock the very foundation that Christianity was based on - the concept of Trinity; he literally broke the Cross and this was all done under the very noses of the British, the self-proclaimed defenders of the Christian faith.

Mirza Ghulam Ahmad(as) brought to the knowledge of all around him the fact that Jesus(as) did not die on the Cross. Everyone was astounded by this claim; the Christians as well as all the other orthodox Muslims, who also believed that Christ was alive in Heaven with God, while Muhammad(sa), their own Prophet, was buried on Earth.

In view of this fantastic claim, was it any wonder then that Mirza Ghulam Ahmad(as) was attacked on all sides, by Christians and Muslims alike. Though the other Muslims discredited him totally and considered the Ahmadis to be outside the pale of Islam, the appearance of Mirza Ghulam Ahmad(as) had a great effect on the state of the dormant Muslims.

How could a man of such humble means, and having no physical power backing him, stand alone and make such incredible claims without any fear of the might of Christianity? In more ways than one, it gave strength and conviction to the other Muslims to sit up and take notice and to guard their faith. A lot of revival movements began a return to fundamentalism and, since then, there has been a general and marked swing towards religious awareness and conservatism. Some have obviously crossed the line and gone overboard.

They see it as their duty to stop the community from sliding into secularism and Westernisation, which they equate with unbelief and immorality, and they have taken on a revolutionary role. Pakistan and Iran are dramatic examples of a universal trend in the world of Islam, and religious conservatism is felt to be a new and powerful force in most of the Muslim world.

DISAPPOINTMENT AND FEAR OF THE WEST

All this must have come as a bitter blow to the Christian nations of the West, whose evil plans and machinations had been thwarted yet again. They must have seriously thought that towards the end of the last century they had done their dirty deed and almost had Islam dead and buried like its Prophet(as), while Christianity appeared to be back in the ascendancy and in the clouds.

But there was worse to follow, for the West that is. The mass migration over the last two to three decades to Britain especially and to some other European countries and America and Canada of ethnic groups from all over the world, has turned the affairs of the West upside-down.

It is true that some of the cultures of the ethnic minorities have been completely swamped by the predominant culture of the West; people from the West Indies, Africa, the Far East and the Indian sub-continent have tried to assimilate into the Western way of life, to be accepted into their society and basically have taken a laissez-faire attitude of 'When in Rome, do as the Romans do'.

Although these immigrants have kept their individual faiths to a point, they have, nevertheless, acquired similar habits in most social areas; for example, the free intermingling of the sexes, the way that they dress, unprohibited drinking, gambling and dancing.

The West had thought, naively perhaps, that the Muslims too would lose their way and their faith and stray from the right path, and that the name of Islam would slowly disintegrate. But sadly for the West, Islam made a dramatic return to fundamentalism - fundamentalism in law, in economy, and especially in culture. This resurgence in Islam, as it were, saw a cultural trend back towards conservatism, not only in Islamic countries, but also in the West as well - right in the heart of the homeland of the Christian nations of the West. The social status of the Imam of the local mosque increased considerably and his views were listened to with the greatest respect.

Another aspect of the fervour in the religious climate was the growth and popularity of religious student unions who organised many of the anti-Western demonstrations. It should be remembered that not all such demonstrations are truly Islamic; however they do reflect the people's strengthening ties with their religion - a feature which gives them a sense of identity.

The status of women had been markedly affected by the return to fundamentalist Islam. The burqa or veil was back in vogue. And despite all the propaganda that the West could muster against the alleged second class citizen status of women in Islam, the rate of conversion to Islam by women in the West in the last decade had reached such high proportions that it had become a most worrying and alarming matter of urgency for the West that needed drastic action.

POINT OF CONTENTION

The main complaint of the British that has been levelled against the ethnic minorities who have come to live and settle in their country, is that the minorities do not do enough to adapt to the ways of the host country so as to be accepted into society, even if it means having to forego some or all of their ancient customs and religious beliefs. This is especially aimed at the British Muslims whom they regard as stubborn and a serious hurdle to establishing a fully Western-orientated cultural society.

The worry and fear of the Muslims for the West is a real one. They know that most Muslims living in the West regard it as a godless society in which Islam provides spiritual guidance that other faiths no longer offer. They are also worried that the muezzins calling the faithful to prayer are drowning the sound of church bells. Most Muslims living in the West are unbending in their determination to preserve their own standards of value and to protect their exclusively Islamic view of the world. Of course, the Muslims want to be liked; they want to fit in; they want to succeed. But they want to be Muslims far more. And this is the sore point that touches the sensitivity of the Christians in the West who are deeply envious of the Muslims' adherence to moral virtues which are sadly lacking or non-existent in the West today.

For people who hold these views against the Muslims, they would do well to heed Roy Hattersley's comments on the subject. Roy Hattersley, a well-respected and popular British Parliamentarian, wrote an article in the Sunday Times (6 June 1993) in which he challenged the views of Winston Churchill on Britain's multi-racial mix and concluded with this observation:

'One thing is certain....the Muslim British are here to stay - stay in Britain and stay steadfastly Muslim in custom and attitude. They will not be assimilated into a secular British society or disappear under a veneer of bogus conformity. We can either celebrate their virtues, build on their strengths and accept their differences, or we can encourage a climate of suspicion, distaste and fear. Common sense, as well as compassion, demands that we rejoice in our new diversity.'

COMPARISON

Let us now put the shoe on the other foot and look at the role of the West, and how far they went to adapt to the customs and beliefs of the countries that they went to and ruled over, and in particular, the role of the Christian missionaries.

The Western missionaries moved into Islamic lands under the protection of the imperial 'umbrella'. This system initially proved to be a great advantage and it enabled missions to take root in Islamic soil. In more recent times, however, it has become a definite liability as Western missionaries are often identified with the now-hated imperialism of the West.

It has always been and still is a characteristic of many Western missionaries, that they tend to congregate in cultural ghettos and make little effort to really get to know the culture of the country that they live in. As Dr. Ali freely admits, and he should know as he is also a Christian missionary who started off in a Muslim country:

'Even though they (Christian missionaries) live in a Muslim country, they continue to behave as if they were still in Western Europe or North America.'

(Islam, A Christian Perspective, p.154).

Dr. Ali also admits to 'the history of imperial domination and colonial exploitation by the West.' (p. 155).

This argument carries more import when it comes from the pen of a Christian missionary who was born in one of the countries that the West had such a big influence on, and is a product of their mission. Dr. Ali continues:

'But while recognising that some expatriates may feel called to identify with the very poor of a particular country, this must not by any means be confused with identifying with the indigenous culture. This assumption itself seems to be a sign of arrogance, implying that the missionary's culture is always superior, and that identification with the host culture involves deprivation ....Many missionaries, however, never go beyond the acquisition of rudimentary knowledge of a local language. They have no real encounter with the art, music and literature of the country in which they live and where they have been called to serve.'

(p. 155).

Dr. Ali is also aware of the 'real danger of creating the kind of nationalist Christianity which, by its very nature, is inward looking and ignorant'. Is it not amazing to note the comparison! When the Western powers went out to the other countries, including Muslim ones, they imposed their superiority as rulers and kept their culture intact and kept their own exclusive social circle; but when the Muslims, together with other groups of people, have come to live in the West and have come to serve and are renowned for being law-abiding citizens, why then are they being singled out for not conforming to the culture and ways of the West and being accused of creating ghettos and living as a closed community? Surely, this is not fair play, is it?

CHAPTER SIX

PLANS TO RECONSTRUCT MUSLIM THOUGHT

Going back to the reconstruction of Muslim thought in colonial India, what the West had tried before was to give the Muslim liberal scholars of that era a free rein in expressing their ways and means of 'Westernising' Islam so that it could be accepted almost as a Muslim apology to the West. Furthermore, what the West cannot deny is their backing to this conniving plan of the reconstruction for Muslim thought. Even Dr. Michael Nazir Ali admits to this in his book, *Islam - A Christian Perspective*:

> 'Turning from the Middle East to India, we find that there Islamic modernism began not as a reaction to European influence but almost under its tutelage.'
>
> (p. 107).

Despite all their efforts and their backing of the plan to liberalise Islam, which had a very hopeful beginning, the plan failed miserably. The major reason may be that liberalism remained the concern of a westernised elite and never succeeded in making any inroads into the ranks of the Ulema (clergy). Another major factor could be, as Dr. Ali admits, that -

'Muslim liberalism of this period was addressed mainly to the European mind. Herein lies one of the causes of its failure within the world of Islam'.

(p. 139).

So the West was in a dilemma. This plan of theirs to reconstruct Muslim thought had almost worked by firstly using their own orientalists, who in a beguiling fashion used their wizardry with the pen to praise the Holy Prophet(sa) on the one hand, and then crucify him on the other. This was aimed more at the Western world, to deter them from appreciating Islam and its beauty, as they were genuinely concerned that people were entering the fold of Islam in their thousands.

Secondly, they targeted the Muslims themselves by using the Muslims' own scholars who showed liberalism in their thinking, and exploiting them to 'soften' the conservatism within their own ranks. As this failed also, a new and more devious plan had to be conjured up; more subtle and more beguiling than all the others put together. And they took their time in making this plan so that it could be damaging to the extreme.

There was a need for a fresh reconstruction of Muslim liberal thought, and this new liberal interpretation of Islam had to provide a cogent alternative to the conservative programme of the Mullah and the extremists.

So who could be the new liberal scholar who would revolutionise Muslim thought to the advantage of the West and Christianity, which was, and still is, in evident decline? Dr. Ali has expressed this need of a new liberal and has outlined his role:

'The new liberal must address himself primarily to the world of Islam and will have to take account of the forces of anti - imperialism which form part of the world today.'

(p. 139).

39

THE NEW LIBERAL 'SCHOLAR'

All the previous works of the orientalists had been for the benefit of religious scholars and the style of writing was complicated and too 'historically' minded. Many of the criticisms and insults levelled at the Holy Prophet(sa) were carefully disguised so that there would be no major outcry, but at the same time they presented a distorted and ambiguous image of Islam. The best way to portray Islam and its noble personages in a negative and flagitious way was to employ the literary craft of a 'fiction' writer who could by his sensational style use it to the maximum effect. Even if things did go wrong, there would always be the 'cushion' of the work being one of fiction!

So the search was on for a suitable candidate who would fit in with the nefarious plans of the West. The final piece in the jigsaw puzzle had to emerge. Ideally, this new liberal should be from an Indian/Pakistani background; he should be a Muslim only in name; he should be a member of the Westernised 'elite'; and if he were an author of some repute, so much the better.

The seeds had been sown years, perhaps centuries ago, and now the poisonous fruit was almost ready. This was to be their 'Ace up the sleeve', who in the end turned out to be the 'Joker in the Pack' - only the facts proved later that it was to be no joke; it was to be no laughing matter for all concerned. In fact it turned out to be quite the opposite. Even non-Muslims all around the world were going to add a new word to their vocabularies no matter what language they spoke - and this word was Fatwa. The scene was set for Salman Rushdie who fulfilled all the requirements adequately. There are bad apples in every cart, but the West had scraped the very bottom to dig out the most rotten one in the shape of Rushdie, and furthermore it has exposed this rotten apple to the rest of the world to suggest that in Islam, these sorts of 'apples' are progressively becoming the norm.

I shall return to this later.

ISLAM'S SELF-SUFFICIENCY

Another criticism levelled against Islam has been its image of being self-sufficient. The Western orientalists have always tried to portray Muslims as being blind in their belief in Islam and its teachings and in Islam being self-sufficient for their moral and secular needs. And because of this, they argue that ordinary Muslims are prevented from gaining any knowledge of doctrines of other faiths. This attitude of trying to prevent people from hearing about other doctrines seems then to show a distrust of the ability of the ordinary human mind to distinguish between truth and falsehood. Montgomery Watt, in his book *Muslim-Christian Encounters*, accusingly dates this thought back to the time of the Holy Prophet(sa):

'There are a number of Hadith and stories of early Muslims which serve to enforce the principle that it is undesirable to have religious discussions with Jews and Christians. When the Caliph Umar came to Muhammad carrying a Jewish or Christian book, the latter was angry.'

(p. 43).

Sir Hamilton Gibb oversteps the mark even further in his book *Modern Trends in Islam* (University of Chicago Press, 1947; p. 125), when he says that the presentation of Islamic history by the Ulema came to be 'invested with religious sanctions, so that to question it came to be regarded as heresy.'

What a distorted and false picture of Islam they have painted. It was Muhammad(sa) himself who showed the greatest practical example of tolerance and respect to people not only of other faiths but also to pagans as well. Not only did he emphasise the desirability of tolerance in religious matters but also he set a very high standard himself. By way of example, it is narrated that:

'A deputation from a Christian tribe of Najran visited him in Medina to exchange views on religious matters. It included several Church dignitaries. The conversation was held in the mosque and extended over several hours. At one stage the leader

41

of the deputation asked permission to depart from the mosque and to hold their religious service at some convenient spot. The Holy Prophet (sa) said that there was no need for them to go out of the mosque, which was itself consecrated to the worship of God, and that they could hold their service in it.'

(Zurqani)

Surely in this incident, which is only one of many that occurred in the life of the Holy Prophet(sa), we can see displayed the height of respect and tolerance never before or since witnessed by any other faith or prophet. It is sheer jealousy of the universality of Islam and its self-efficiency that haunts and hurts the Christians and their true fear is also expressed by Watt who says:

'This lack of interest in everything other than Islam and the Islamic world is not surprising when one remembers the picture of world-history developed by Muslim scholars out of Qur'anic perceptions. Since Muhammad was the final Prophet and Islam the final religion, the historical process must be moving towards the ultimate triumph of Islam throughout the world. This meant that Christianity would probably fade away compltely.'

(Muslim-Christian Encounters, page 49.)

Perhaps this was the fear and the reason that gave birth to the Western Orientalists. As Watt freely admits in the same book:

'Many of the European colonialist writings about Islam had the aim of getting to understand it better, in order to control it better...... The Christians, for their part, formed a number of separate groups under the colonialist power.... It would have been imprudent of them to make serious criticisms of Islam openly, or to form a distorted image of it, such as was created in Western Europe.'

(pp. 72-73).

It is interesting to note Watt's comments as he is regarded as one of the giants among the Western Orientalists; and here he categorically states that the aim of the orientalists had been to 'control' Islam,

42

implying that Islam was getting out of hand and was spreading world-wide. He further admits that Western critics of Islam had created a 'distorted' image of it in Europe.

CHAPTER SEVEN

THE WESTERN ORIENTALISTS

I will briefly look at a few of the Western orientalists of this century and compare their works and it will become evident from these works that their source seems to be the same and that the same accusations are made against Islam, the Holy Prophet(sa), his Companions, the Holy Qur'an, the Hadith; in fact, all the distinctive features and characteristics faintly connected with Islam are put to ridicule.

What is also evident is the beguiling way that they present this - in one instance they pass a complimentary remark about the Holy Prophet(sa) and in the very next one they crucify him. This hypocrisy in their writing is an in-built trait and has been employed since the very early literary attacks on Islam.

MAXIME RODINSON

Maxime Rodinson, a French Orientalist, was the son of the founder of the Jewish Workers Trade Union in Paris. Rodinson later joined the Communist Party and became an Atheist. His most famous and polemic work is in the form of a book simply titled *Mohammed*. This book is a study of the impact of the ideology of Islam upon the society of 7th century Arabia.

In it he places Prophet Muhammad's achievements in the context of his time. But interspersed in it are defamatory and calumnious attacks on his character and on other noble personages of Islam.

Even Muhammad's conception is given a titillating effect where his father is regarded as sex-hungry, going from one wife to another for gratification. (p. 42).

Details of Muhammad's childhood are made to be unreliable and are referred to as 'legends' to fill the void and which became more beautiful and edified with the passage of time. (p. 143).

Rodinson writes that before prophethood Muhammad(sa) 'practiced the religion of his fathers.. and we are told that he sacrificed a sheep to the goddess al-'Uzza.' (p. 48). The Hadith are regarded as 'fictitious', and he also uses the word 'forged' about them.

ALLEGATIONS AGAINST THE PROPHET

Muhammad(sa) is called mad, a mystic, a kahin (soothsayer), a revolutionary, and one having fits and being epileptic. (pp. 53-57).

Rodinson also mentions that '18th century rationalist philosophers for instance, like Christian apologists and theologians, looked on Muhammad as the example of a perfect fraud.' (p. 76).

The state of Arabia at the inception of Islam is, without doubt, regarded as one of the worst in the history of the world and what the critics have tried to convey is that some of the evil influences must have rubbed off on Muhammad(sa) and his Companions for them to survive. As Rodinson mentions further:

'The times he (Muhammad) lived in, and the rough nature of the Arabs he had to lead obliged him to resort to fraud if he was to make any impression on such people.'

(p. 76).

With reference to the battles in the early years of Islam, Muhammad(sa) is made out to be the aggressor and one who showed no mercy for his captives, and one who would resort to anything to achieve his goal. Rodinson states:

'The volunteer who undertook his assassination explained to the Prophet that it would be necessary to resort to cunning, trickery and lies. Muhammad saw no objection.'

(p. 176).

Muhammad(sa) is made out to be a man who had no patience and was always susceptible to anger and consequent barbaric actions against his enemies:

'We have seen that Muhammad had at his disposal a number of fanatical young henchmen, who were virtually prepared to strike down any opposition whenever necessary.'

(pp. 223-224).

Similarly he writes:

'Muhammad allowed his henchmen a free rein.'

(p. 184).

How low indeed Rodinson has stooped to give spurious and feigned accounts of facts and incidents in the life of the Holy Prophet(sa) of Islam.

Maxime Rodinson is no different from other orientalists of the same coalescence when he jumps on the bandwagon and accuses the Holy Prophet(sa) of being licentious. He is alleged to have had desires for young and beautiful women:

'Even so, knowing what we do of his amorous proclivities later on in life, we can scarcely imagine that there were not plenty of times when he... committed adultery in his heart.'

(p. 55).

The West has, with very few honourable exceptions, through 14 centuries ignored all that was patently good and beneficent in the life of the Holy Prophet(sa) and in Islam and, when confronted by his example and his doctrine, has taken shelter behind flimsy and untenable excuses.

One of the favourite subjects of the Western orientalists has been to persistently level calumnies at the Holy Prophet(sa) that in his later life he became licentious. That is an enormity that has only to be contemplated to be immediately rejected as utterly incompatible with his life and character. The affirmation that polygamy negates high spirituality carries no weight. It should be remembered that in none of the great religious systems has polygamy been forbidden in the scriptures of a religion. All the Jewish prophets, including Moses(as), had a plurality of wives. No one has ever alleged that because of this they could not be accounted as leading virtuous lives.

This subject has become one of ridicule and titillation on the part of the mischief-makers, namely the Western orientalists, who have channelled this view and portrayal to the world. The Western scholars who have expressed honourable views through logical and rational thinking are not fully exposed to the masses and their writings go relatively unnoticed. For example, Professor Laura Veccia Vaglieri, at one time Professor of Arabic and Islamic Culture in the University of Naples, has observed:

'Enemies of Islam have insisted in depicting Muhammad as a sensual individual and a dissolute man, trying to find in his marriages evidence of a weak character not consistent with his mission. They refuse to take into consideration the fact that during those years of his life when by nature the sexual urge is strongest, although he lived in a society like that of the Arabs, .. where polygamy was the rule, and where divorce was very easy indeed, he was married to one woman alone, Khadija, who was much older than himself, and that for twenty-five years he was her faithful, loving husband. Only when she died and when he was already more than fifty years old did he marry again and more than once. Each of these marriages had a social or political reason,... With the sole exception of Aisha, he married women who were neither virgins, nor young nor beautiful. Was this sensuality?'

(An Interpretation of Islam, pp. 67-68).

One of the main reasons the Holy Prophet(sa) married Aisha was to enable her to guide people on Islam, especially women, throughout her lifetime. She performed this task exceptionally well and proved to be a tremendous source of guidance for a long time, not only during the life of the Holy Prophet(sa) but also afterwards. Such was Muhammad's wisdom.

Sir Muhammad Zafrulla Khan, an eminent Ahmadi scholar in world religions, delves deeper in his analogous rational argument in favour of the nobility of the character of the Holy Prophet(sa), thus dispelling any doubts as to the calumnies levelled at the noblest of God's creatures. In an excellent appraisal of the life of Muhammad(sa) in his renowned book *Muhammad - Seal of the Prophets*, he argues thus:

'Except for his marriage to Sudah, a pious, aged, indigent widow, all the Holy Prophet's subsequent marriages took place after his migration to Medina. How was he occupied in Medina and what was the type of life that he led there? Even the most casual reader.... would be deeply impressed with his heavy responsibilities, his diligent discharge of them, his preoccupation with the teachings of the faith to his followers, ministering to them as their spiritual preceptor, leading the five daily Prayer services, administering the affairs of the heterogeneous population of Medina, spending the greater part of his night in voluntary Prayer; and would wonder how much of his time was spent in the company of his wives, and how that time was employed by him.... the Holy Prophet's own life was a model not only of simplicity, but even of rigorous asceticism. He permitted no indulgence of any kind to himself or to his wives..... Aisha is reported to have said that the Holy Prophet(sa) was more modest than a virgin. Would that be the description of a person who was consumed with carnal passion and sought every opportunity for the satisfaction of his sensual desires through marrying a large number of women?'

(p. 280).

48

ATTACKS ON THE HOLY QUR'AN

Maxime Rodinson continues his assault on Islam by casting doubts on the purity of the Holy Qur'an. He gives more regard to the work of the European Orientalists rather than the Muslim commentators of the Holy Qur'an. He seems to be an ardent fan of Theodor Noldeke, the German Semitic scholar, who 'has written at length about the stylistic defects of the Koran.' (p. 93).

He further implies that the Qur'an had been revised under the direction of Muhammad(sa) and gives the view of the Christian rationalists that 'Muhammad was guilty of falsification, by deliberately attributing to Allah his own thoughts and instructions', (p. 218), and 'nudging the truth a little.' (p. 78).

This then allegedly gave rise to the satanic influences in some of the verses, as Rodinson writes:

'It is obvious to non-Muslims that the words which Muhammad heard, by which his experiences (in themselves almost inexpressible) were translated in so miraculously perfect a fashion, were dictated to him by his unconscious. He himself suspected it; he had doubted their source, he was afraid that human inspiration might have formed some part of it, and, as we have seen, he even admitted at a later stage that Satan himself had managed to insert his own orders.'

(p. 219).

Rodinson has admitted that in his book he has given an appreciation of Muhammad(sa) on purely objective terms. But the reasons for writing the book are exposed both in the Foreword to the book and in the conclusion.

In the Foreword, he gives some sort of justification for writing a book on Muhammad(sa) when so many of them had already been written, especially recently. The reason surely is that the constant and continuous onslaught against Islam has taken on a deportment of perpetuity. These attacks have to continue in one form or another

49

and what better way than to discredit the Holy Prophet(sa) of Islam and make him out to be whatever takes their fancy, and in showing him, in not just a less than pure light, but in insolent and contemptuous language.

Towards the end of the book, Rodinson puts his foot right in it and shows his true colours when summing up the character of Muhammad(sa). The Promised Messiah(as) had forewarned the Muslims of the bigotry of the Western scholars in his book *Victory of Islam*, when he said that the Christian nations of the West would use beguiling and cunning ways to lead people astray by using lies and fabrications.

Mark the ambiguity in Rodinson's language in the last two paragraphs when describing Muhammad's life-sketch:

'The picture is not a simple one. It is neither the satanic monster of some... neither the cold-blooded impostor nor the political theorist, nor the mystic wholly in love with God. If we have understood him rightly, Muhammad was a complex man, full of contradictions. He was fond of his pleasures, yet indulged in bouts of asceticism. He was often compassionate, yet sometimes cruel.... He was cool and nervous, brave and timid, a mixture of cunning and frankness, forgiving and at the same time capable of terrible vindictiveness, proud and humble, chaste and sensual, intelligent and, in certain things, oddly stupid.'

(p. 313).

The sorcery of the orientalists is clearly exposed and it is this very necromancy that has attributed weaknesses on the part of Muhammad(sa) which allegedly have been responsible for satanic influences to enter his mind as they do the minds of ordinary human beings. This is what Maxime Rodinson has adjudged and drawn an inference in his concluding paragraph which also ends in extremely condescending terms:

'Ought we to be surprised at these complexities and contradictions, this mixture of strength and weakness? He was after all, a man like other men, subject to the same weaknesses and sharing the same powers, Muhammad ibn Abdallah of the tribe of Quraysh, our brother.'

(p. 313).

Brother indeed! With a brother like Rodinson, who needs enemies?

DR. NORMAN DANIEL

Dr. Daniel was a scholar of Queen's College, Oxford before the Second World War and later became a protégé of the great Western Orientalist, William Montgomery Watt, after the War. Watt became the supervisor of his doctoral thesis.

With a supervisor like Watt it was no wonder then that his subsequent works should be a parody of Watt's literary contribution to the Muslim-Christian polemic.

Dr. Daniel's most famous work was in keeping with the theme of the Western Orientalists in trying to ascertain why a deformed image of Islam had been established in the European mind and it is this that Dr. Daniel tries to delineate in its process of becoming one of the dogmas of Christian society. But it soon becomes evident that the line of action is the same; the arguments are the same; the very limited source of material is the same, and the dubious motives that surface are also the same. This work by Dr. Daniel is called *Islam and the West - The Making of an Image*, published in 1960. In this book Dr. Daniel studies the formation of the Western idea of Islam during the period 1100-1350.

IMAGE OF ISLAM (1100-1350)

Dr. Daniel starts by mentioning the popular twisted image of Islam during this period; for example, doubts were cast on the authenticity of the Holy Qur'an as being the revealed word of God and the traditions related in the Hadith, and more so doubts were cast on the purity of the character of the Holy Prophet(sa).

51

What was in vogue during this period between the 12th and 14th centuries was 'the tests of Prophethood', whereby standards were set as a yardstick and prophets could be judged according to them.

If perchance, the Christian polemic could show Muhammad(sa) not to be a prophet, then the whole Islamic fabric would have failed. Dr. Daniel observes furthermore, that the reverse would also be true.

In other words, if the Christian polemic could not disprove Muhammad(sa) as a true prophet, then Islam would be a real threat to Christendom. So in order to make sure that Muhammad was to be wholly discredited as a true prophet, the proof that 'Muhammad claimed the title falsely had to be explicit.' (p. 67).

This task came gratefully to the Christian writers. Dr. Daniel quotes Peter the Venerable and especially Pedro de Alfonso and Peter of Poitiers whose collective schemes could be summarised to show that 'Muhammad could not be a prophet, because he was a robber, a murderer, a traitor and an adulterer' and also that the teachings of the Qur'an were 'shameful and contradictory' and 'not being confirmed by miracles.' (p 68).

Dr. Daniel continues:

'The life of Muhammad was seen as an essential disproof of the Islamic claim to Revelation. It was often treated as the most important disproof of all. To this end writers believed and wished to show that Muhammad was a low-born and pagan upstart, who schemed himself into power, who maintained it by pretended revelations, and who spread it both by violence and by permitting to others the same lascivious practices as he indulged in himself.'

(p. 79).

For all Dr. Daniel's attempts to delineate the deformed image of Islam through the works of other Western Orientalists, he himself has fallen prey to the dogmas of the Christian Church, and this is clearly manifested when he implies in his writing that there must be some truth in the allegations against Muhammad(sa) if everyone else is making the same insinuations:

'In all the accounts of Muhammad's life which have some relation to reality, but omitting the wholly fabulous, two consistent themes dominate all that is said. Muhammad was violent; he levied war and ordered assassinations unscrupulously for private ends, for plunder, and even more for ambition. Secondly, he was subject to human frailty; he had his ups and downs, a history which revealed the ordinary fluctuations of fortune.'

(p. 96).

Daniel also follows the path of previous Orientalists when he alleges lasciviousness to the character of Muhammad(sa). Several pages are expended in pursuit of this, but I shall quote just one example, which is hurtful enough to relate, but which will no doubt give the reader a sample of the malicious and vindictive writing of the author:

'Probably the favourite mediaeval story of Muhammad was that of his marriage to Zaynab bint Jahsh after her divorce from Zayd ibn Haritha. The story has popular appeal of a police-court character...: the all but incestuous adultery with the wife of an adopted son; Muhammad's inability to resist fleshly temptation; the use of a special revelation to justify what he had done.'

(p. 97).

So with all these accusations and assertions by the Christian polemic of that period, it came as no surprise when the medieval Christians came to the conclusion that Muhammad's (alleged) behaviour with women alone made it quite impossible that he should have been a prophet.

DEATH OF THE PROPHET

Dealing with the subject of the death of the Holy Prophet(sa), varying and incredible accounts had been concocted.

As deaths of the saints were thought specially significant by their biographers, and in medieval tradition the death of Muhammad(sa), the antithesis of the saint, was considered a subject of theological importance, it was often shown as having been atrociously horrible, sometimes simply as just having been of a normal human being, with no signs of God's special mercy.

Some of these falsifications are too painful to divulge and to inflict them on any reader in any sort of detail would be sacrilege. Those wishing to read at length the different stories concocted by the Christian writers relating to the manner of the death of the Holy Prophet(sa) should read the relevant section in Dr. Daniel's book. (pp. 102-107).

Dr. Daniel's hypocrisy is evident when he admits to the credibility of some of the stories. The main aim to portray an ignominious death of the Holy Prophet(sa) was to taint him with unsaintly qualities. As Dr. Daniel writes:

'As a good death marks the saint, so the Prophet was allotted an appropriate, and usually an appropriately horrible, one. This was inevitably so, in order to seal his unsanctity.'

(p. 106-107).

SELF-INDULGENCE

The attacks on Islam continue with reference to its alleged self-indulgence. This topic finds a peculiar interest to the point of fetishism with the Western reader, both of yesteryear and of the present. Even Dr. Daniel states that where morals of sex were concerned:

'it was felt that this subject was as important for the welfare of Christendom as it was inherently stimulating to the imagination of individuals. The Christian criticism and exaggeration of the license attributed to Muslims was often excessive.'

(p. 135).

Dr. Daniel further admits to the true motives of the orientalists and also to the source of the so-called 'facts' that are often quoted as being from the same school of thought and research:

'All writers tended - more or less - to cling to fantastic tales about Islam and its Prophet in a proprietary way, as belonging to the 'Christian' version....Those 'facts' which tended to show the falsity of Islam were preferred to all others. The same polemic outline is common to the more scholarly and the more popular works. There was a rough unity of purpose and a similar attitude to the use of data. The difference lay only in degree. More that was incredible was excluded, more that was authentic admitted, in one case than in the next. The use of false evidence to attack Islam was all but universal.'

(p240/241).

Dr. Daniel, like his contemporaries, expresses unequivocally the real reason for this 'falsification' and the real fear of the Christians that Islam was beginning to appeal to the West:

'The Middle Ages were like other ages in inventing and re-arranging the facts of history and the beliefs of opponents in order to suit some noble purpose. It is important to realise that the facts and the Islamic doctrines thus rearranged were put into a form which primarily repelled, and must have been intended to repel, Christians; Islam was, in fact, not always described in terms necessarily repellent to Muslims. No doubt there was much that a Muslim would have had to resent; but the unpleasant image of Islam that the Christians drew was drawn to seem unpleasant to the Christian eye...... In one way and another Islam was made to seem repellent, either as unlike or else as actually contrary to all the most important Christian teaching.'

(pp. 264-265).

Even the hardened critics of Islam, like Dr. Daniel, cannot deny the above-mentioned facts, and he has time and again had to admit to the fear and jealousy of the Christians. Another example follows soon after:

'Islam was still at the frontier. For this reason it had to be admitted openly as an enemy, and presented in terms that did not make it necessary to change or adapt any single facet of Christian and European culture..... The important thing was that it suited the West. It corresponded to need; it made it possible to protect the minds of Christians against apostasy and it gave Christendom self-respect in dealing with a civilisation in many ways its superior.'

(p. 270).

COERCIVE EFFIGY

One of the most popular myths that has been created about Islam and how it was spread was the assertion that it was spread by force, and by the sword. No credit has been vouchsafed to the superior and compassionate teachings of the Holy Qur'an as elucidated by the Holy Prophet(sa). This false picture of conversion by coercion had been deliberately painted to stem the rate of converts from the Christian faith to Islam.

But this picture was literally presented as a drawing in this period and the Western orientalists have taken advantage of every opportunity to present it to the world.

Muslims, throughout the centuries, and right up to the present time, have always regarded their Prophet(sa) with such reverence that no paintings or drawings of him have ever been made or been permitted. But some of the orientalists have displayed great insensitivity by doing exactly the opposite.

Dr. Daniel has joined this category of insensitive writers by digging out one such drawing and presenting it in his book. The notes accompanying it are equally callous. Daniel calls it 'an ink drawing of Muhammad, from a late mediaeval manuscript, where it stands in isolation - it was apparently not intended to illustrate a text.' (p. 134).

56

The drawing depicts Muhammad(sa) carrying a sword in the right hand, with the words "gladius Mahumeti pictus" written across it, and holding a Qur'an in the left hand, with the words "lex et alcoranus" written on it : this is the mythical image that has been portrayed by the enemies of Islam.

There are also talismans hanging from the collar of Muhammad(sa), implying that he was a sorcerer and an exorcist who used his magic spell to convert people!

If this was not enough, Dr. Daniel has the audacity and effrontery to suggest that the 'treatment is dignified'! One shudders to think if this was a 'dignified' portrayal of Muhammad(sa), what would be the result if an undignified depiction was really undertaken!

SIMILARITY OF THE ORIENTALISTS

It seems that the real motive of the Orientalists to study Islam and, in particular, the life of Muhammad(sa), has been to present a distorted image as has been too plain to see. Almost all the writers seem to have banded together using the same limited sources which they have exploited time and again, so much so that they are beginning to sound like worn-out records.

The way that they have presented the background of Muhammad's life, the Arabia into which he was born, his own early life, his call to Prophethood and the circumstances of his death, were all presented as demonstrating that he was human, fallible and subject to every discreditable misfortune. (In fact, this is exactly the method employed by Salman Rushdie in his infamous novel).

The Orientalists over the years had the habit of quoting former authorities on the same topics, so limited was their source. As Dr. Daniel himself quotes from a book by Reland, a French Orientalist, called *De Religione Mohammedica* [The religion of Mohammad] (1705):

'If ever any Religion was perverted by Adversarys, it was this Religion (Islam); it was the custom to send a young man

57

fir'd with a generous Ardor of understanding the Mahometan
Religion to study the old authorities, including Ketton, instead
of advising him to learn the Arabick, to hear Mahomet speak in
his own tongue.'

(p. 295).

Reland established the principle that the sole authority for facts about
Islam must be Muslim, and this point had also been made more than
half a century earlier by Edward Pocock the Elder.

Dr. Daniel sums up by saying that most of the literary attacks
which started during the medieval period have proved extremely
durable and still have a bearing on present-day Western thinking:

> 'Throughout the near fourteen centuries of Islam, Christians
> have defended their faith in the Trinity and Incarnation from
> Muslim attack; and they have in turn attacked Islam for accepting
> the claim of Muhammad to be the vehicle of Revelation, chiefly
> on the grounds that his character made it impossible reasonably
> to do so. Finally they have had to decide upon the admixture of
> truth and error: how to estimate its value, how to allow for the
> error, how to balance judgement upon the significance of each,
> and how to assess the final result. In respect of these points the
> mediaeval concept proved extremely durable; this outline of it
> is still a part of the cultural inheritance of the West to-day.'

(p. 275).

PROFESSOR WILLIAM MONTGOMERY WATT

Of all the modern-day Western Orientalists, surely without doubt,
the most renowned is Montgomery Watt, Emeritus Professor of
Arabic and Islamic studies at the University of Edinburgh. He has
been dubbed 'one of the last of the orientalist giants'. He has written
several books on Islam and the Holy Prophet(sa) including
Muhammad at Mecca, *Muhammad at Medina*, *Muslim - Christian
Encounters*, and *Islamic Fundamentalism and Modernity*.

Watt has become the major present-day component of the
armoury of the West in its struggle against Islam and has become

the scourge of Muslims all over the world. His work and research has been admired and esteemed by all the other Western Orientalists and the greatest tribute they pay to him is by using his same beguiling ways of sowing seeds of doubt and contempt within the structure of Islam in their books; and they have tried desperately to taint the character of the Holy Prophet(sa) and his noble Companions, and they have tried to find inconsistencies in the Holy Qur'an and the traditions of Hadith.

What Montgomery Watt has presented is nothing new compared to the Western scholars before him, but it is the way that he has presented it - just as the Promised Messiah(as) had prophesied:

'in ways most subtle.....all directed to beguile and lead people astray.'

(Victory of Islam, p. 3).

Sir Hamilton Gibb, in the Hibbert-Journal while giving an appreciation of Watt's book *Muhammad at Mecca*, unwittingly remarks that:

'The book gives the impression of having been written by one who has entered imaginatively into the experience of Muhammad in Mecca to a greater degree than any previous biographer.'

And this has been the root cause of the main problem and has been the point of contention - the orientalists, especially the Western ones, have let their 'imaginations' run wild and have based their arguments on hearsay and they have twisted the facts to their advantage, shaping the character of Muhammad(sa) to suit their own passions, ideas and fantasies.

By way of example, I will just mention a few instances. In his book *Islamic Fundamentalism and Modernity*, Watt has even doubted 'the traditional Islamic conception of the Qur'an as the word of God', and talks of 'the human element in its revelation.' (p. 82). I am sure the reader will observe that this has been repeated so often by other Western scholars as well.

Watt also talks of errors of historical fact found in the Qur'an, like the one:

'that Mary the mother of Jesus is apparently confused with Miriam the sister of Aaron (19:28); both would be Maryam in Arabic. More important is the apparent denial that Jesus was crucified and died on the Cross (4:157), and the assertion that Christians worship three gods.'

(4:171, 5:73,116) (p. 83).

No book of Montgomery Watt would be complete without the customary attack on the character of the Holy Prophet(sa) and he does not disappoint the Western reader as he writes:

'the idealisation of Muhammad and early Islamic society is also of dubious truth. Muhammad must have shared in the un-Islamic beliefs of his fellow Meccans when he was a young man.'

(p. 86).

Muhammad(sa) is made out to be a man who did not keep his word when faced with adversity. For example, in *Muhammad at Medina*, Watt writes:

'It was of course, one of the sacred months in which there was supposed to be no bloodshed, but Muhammad had not shown himself specially observant of sacred times.'

(p. 47).

Watt has continued to stress in all his books that Muhammad(sa) was the aggressor and spread his religion by the sword and by force. In the same book he writes:

'Sometimes Muhammad encouraged energetic men to use force against their neighbours. One was Surad b. Abdallah of the tribe of Azd Shanu'ah, who came to Muhammad with a dozen or so men; Muhammad put him in charge of these men... and gave them *carte blanche* to fight in the name of Islam against any non-Muslims in the region.'

(p. 120).

Watt has certainly been the stalwart for the West in the last few decades and he certainly has had his say in more ways than one and has almost tired himself out, as he himself freely admits in the preface to *Muhammad at Medina*:

> 'I have said my say about Muhammad, and, if I try to say more, am as likely to mar as to better the impression I have tried to convey.'

Perhaps we should be grateful to Watt for this reprieve! If, by writing his books to date, he has been trying to convey a good impression of Muhammad(sa), then I shudder to think what he could do if he really put his mind to marring the character of Muhammad(sa)!

CHAPTER EIGHT

NEW BREED OF 'SCHOLARS'

To replace Watt would be a really difficult task for the Christian scholars in the West; they must have explored all sorts of avenues and possibilities; they had even begun to find scholars from within the Indo-Pakistani Muslim community; perhaps this was to be their future plan: to find infiltrators from within these communities and, slowly but surely, to expose them to the West.

DR. MICHAEL NAZIR-ALI

The first of these was Dr. Michael Nazir-Ali, a former Provost of Lahore Cathedral in Pakistan, and who presently has become the first Asian Diocese Bishop in England. He was bestowed this honour in January 1995.

Dr. Nazir-Ali was born in Pakistan and came from a Muslim background but converted to Christianity with his father at an early age. He has been living in England for most of his adult life so he was an ideal tool for the West to exploit and he was fully 'encouraged' to write on Islam from a Christian viewpoint.

Dr. Ali has borrowed most of his material from previous orientalists and some liberal-minded Muslim scholars; therefore what he presented was nothing really new or startling. His first book which he wrote in 1980 is entitled *Islam - A Christian Perspective*, in which he clearly expresses the Christians' jealousy of Muhammad's reverence and adoration by his followers compared to that of any other Prophet, including Jesus. The jealousy continues to seep out throughout the book and he is brave enough to suggest that the God of the Christians is better than the one mentioned in the Qur'an:

> 'the Qur'an always speaks of God's love for the righteous or for the believers and never of his love for sinners. The New Testament, on the other hand, speaks often of God's love for sinners.'
>
> (p. 62).

SIMILAR ATTACKS

In trying to sway the argument in his favour, he acts no differently to the other Christian scholars who found the 'easy way out' by attacking the Holy Prophet(sa) of Islam with great untruths and twisted accounts and narrations. For example, in the space of a short paragraph, he sums up the age-old accusations levelled against Muhammad(sa) with regard to him being licentious and cruel. Dr. Ali writes:

> 'The whole pattern of Muhammad's life was thoroughly Arab: his plurality of wives, his concubines, his raiding (razzia) of laden caravans in times of poverty, his unpredictable cruelty as well as his sudden generosity....all these were deeply ingrained into Muhammad's character.'
>
> (p. 24).

Dr. Ali is also in unison with the other Western scholars and attributes satanic thoughts to Muhammad(sa):

> 'This may account for his original acceptance of the goddesses Lat, Manat and 'Uzza as intercessors with Allah. He said later that this verse had been inspired by Satan, and changed it!'
>
> (p. 25).

The author continues on the offensive against the character of the Holy Prophet(sa):

'the disturbing thing is that Muhammad married eleven wives in violation of the very revelation which he claimed to have received', and again, 'the famous saying about the prophet that he loved three things: prayer, perfume and women!'

(pp. 32-33).

There is a lot of other material of the same kind that can be found throughout the book, and as it is painful enough to quote even one of them, I do not think that I should tarry any longer in this direction. It suffices to say that this work by Dr. Ali had 'deja-vu' written all over it, but as far as the spiteful plan of the West was concerned, this work was not nearly strong enough nor damaging enough to cause any ripples or make any waves of any significance. It was too tame and hardly controversial.

Something more dramatic and more sensational had to be plotted; something that would make everyone sit up and take notice. This would be the culmination of all the plotting and machinations devised by the two major enemies of Islam, namely the Jews and the Christians. Before we get to the end result of this plan, let me first bring the reader up to date on some of the other factors that contributed to the fruition of this plan.

CONTEMPORARY ATTACKS

The West had still not managed to penetrate the conservative thinking within Islam; so seeds of doubt, in some way or another, had to be sown within those ranks, and the Christian nations were also aware of a small, but mainly silent body of liberal opinion in Islam which they had tried desperately to exploit. The Sharia is made out to be medieval in its moral guidance and that little, if anything, had been done to adapt it to the new social structures of life at the end of the 20th century. The hopes and aspirations of the Western Orientalists are fully exposed in the concluding paragraph of Watt's *Islamic Fundamentalism and Modernity*, (p. 143):

64

'When ordinary Muslims become aware that the idyllic conditions they were promised if they went back to early Islam are unlikely to be realised in practice, there may be a greater revulsion of feeling against those who advocate that policy.'

But how wrongly and gravely they made their judgements and how it backfired on them! Watt was right in assuming that there 'may be a greater revulsion of feeling', but only it turned out to be against the very people who had tried to instil this kind of thought - and that was the West.

CHAPTER NINE

NEW WORLD ORDER

Another major contemporary reason for the West to destroy Islam could well be derived from this viewpoint. It is no guarded secret that the superpowers of today have a dream of a 'New World Order', the head of which would be the USA, admittedly the most powerful nation in the world today. According to the thinking in the West, the development of science and technology has meant that the human race is moving towards a single world order. There is already a degree of political unification in the United Nations, albeit a cosmetic one in nature and totally ineffective in justly solving any problems.

There is also a movement towards a single world intellectual culture, which is still far from being unified. Most of the world's nations are accepting the secular aspect of Western intellectual culture, but beyond that there is considerable diversity, especially in the field of religion. The realisation of the aims of this movement towards a unified world culture means that all the religions have to re-examine their attitudes towards this emerging unity, especially fundamentalist Islam. In fact, they would prefer all the religions to make compromises as their aim for the foreseeable future is a comity of religions. The all-powerful, all-forceful West is presenting this new order to the world and 'inviting' all to have a share in it, by contributing to it. The fear they have of Islam is that Islam boasts of self-sufficiency and that it is spreading like wild-fire amongst the nations of the world, including the West.

Up until the birth of Islam, Christianity went relatively unchallenged and was able to spread to almost all parts of the world with the teaching that through Christ alone was the one and only way to salvation, and that Christianity was superior to all other faiths.

It would seem now, that since the unprecedented spread of Islam, especially into Europe, it has made the Christians sit up and take notice of Islam's very real threat to their plans of world dominance; and now being the Muslims' turn to preach that Islam is the one and only true light to the right path, the ball is very much in Islam's court.

To control this 'problem', as it certainly had become one for the Christian nations, they pushed forward even more forcibly this idea of an emerging united world culture with the observation that all religions show that they are all doing more or less the same thing anyway, with similar aims! Therefore, this way of thinking would leave no room for the adherents of any faith to consider itself to be superior to that of another. It was almost, on the part of the Christian nations, like an act of abject surrender. Even Watt in his book, *Muhammad at Medina*, makes this very interesting and noteworthy observation:

'The world is becoming increasingly one world, and in this one world there is a tendency towards unification and uniformity. Because of this tendency the day will doubtless come when there will be a set of moral principles which not merely claim universal validity but are actually accepted almost universally throughout the one world. Now Muslims claim that Muhammad is a model of conduct and character for all mankind. In doing so they invite world opinion to pass judgement upon him. Up till now the matter has received scant attention from world opinion, but, because of the strength of Islam, it will eventually have to be given serious consideration.'

(p. 333).

The truth of the matter is that the character of Muhammad(sa) and the religion of Islam has been receiving a lot of attention, especially in the last century, and that it has been given the most serious of considerations, but all for the wrong reasons!

MUHAMMAD'S CHARACTER MALIGNED

The Western orientalists, especially Watt, have fully availed themselves of all the material which depicts the life of Muhammad(sa) in the minutest detail. Muhammad's life was an open book for everyone to read freely. Never in the history of mankind have the actions and sayings of a single person been looked at with such scrutiny as have been those of the Holy Prophet(sa) of Islam. The real aim of the western scholars has never been to study the character of Muhammad(sa) to appreciate it fully, but it has been to find faults in any form whatsoever. When they did not succeed in this design, they then twisted the information with deceit and guile. They became so desperate and so focussed to this end that certain Western orientalists devoted their whole work to it. So much so, in fact, that they ended up imagining themselves to be in Muhammad's shoes and thinking like him and putting their own base and spurious ideas and thoughts and passing them off as those of Muhammad(sa).

The real problem is that of jealousy; they could never conceive of anyone being so perfect, and so to make sure that the rest of the non-Muslim world did not fall under the spell of this 'magician', this 'perfect human being', they began to attribute moral lapses and errors of judgement on his part and made him out to be like any ordinary human being. These alleged 'moral lapses' were then gradually led to contribute to him inventing revelations of his own and attributing them to God - thus the idea of the 'satanic verses' was invented.

SATANIC INFLUENCES

The Holy Qur'an, like the character of the Holy Prophet(sa), has had the greatest amount of scrutiny impressed upon it. It has been examined probingly, verse by verse, word by word, by commentators and scholars both Muslim and non-Muslim. But the aim of the Christian and Jewish scholars has been to find inconsistencies, contradictions and historical factual errors at any cost, even if it meant by lying and deceiving.

In this regard, the Jews especially, have taken the lead role through a real sense of jealousy and envy. Muhammad's claim to receive messages from God conflicted with their cherished belief that the Jews were the chosen people through whom alone God revealed Himself to men.

This jealousy probably gave rise to another reason why the opponents of Islam ascribed satanic thoughts to Muhammad(sa): so that the Holy Book of Muslims is not given the 'Divine Seal of Approval'. Even Hans Kung admits to this 'faux pas' by the western scholars in his book *Christianity and the World Religions* while discussing whether the Qur'an is God's Word or not:

> 'And not just Christians, but later on the secular-minded Western religious scholars, who have automatically read the Qur'an not as God's word, but Muhammad's.'
>
> (p. 29).

Even Watt himself criticises the Western orientalists for their unbalanced criticisms of Islam in *Muslim-Christian Encounters*, (p. 115) :

> 'While much of what they (the orientalists) said was true, they failed to balance their criticisms of Islam by any positive appreciation of the values and achievements of Islam as a religion. It is thus not altogether surprising that Muslims should become hostile to orientalists.'

BACKGROUND TO WESTERNISED 'ELITE'

All the arguments so far have, in one way or another, through the passage of time and historical facts, wittingly or, as in some cases unwittingly, directed us to the birth of the present day breed of Rushdies.

Re-assessing the situation, if we go back to the turn of the last century in India, with the Western Colonial presence, the influence of liberal ideas and the consequent reconstruction of Muslim religious thought backed by the Western power behind the Christian missionary movement, there were a great number of conversions from Islam to Christianity. Nevertheless, there were also a lot of other people who did not actually cross the line from Islam to Christianity, but having become dissatisfied with their cultural milieu, wished to challenge it. They did not wish to remain within their racial, linguistic or class setting. They felt ashamed of their own culture and had an inferiority complex. Although they were Muslims by name, that is where their association with Islam ceased. Their thinking and outlook was totally Westernised and their main ambition was to be accepted into the Western way of life. These then were the new class of Western-educated people, most of whom did not accept the traditional Islamic worldview. These were the so-called 'Westernised elite', whence came the family of Salman Rushdie.

PART II

CHAPTER TEN

SALMAN RUSHDIE -
A BRIEF LIFE-SKETCH

Salman Rushdie was born in Bombay, India in June 1947, two months before Indian Independence which led to the creation of the separate Muslim state of Pakistan. His paternal grandfather, Khaliqui Dehlavi, was a doctor and successful businessman in Old Delhi. He was a minor essayist in Urdu and a patron of poets. Dehlavi elected to rename himself 'Rushdie' after an intellectual Arab philosopher he admired. Perhaps the name contained a prophesy, for the Arab philosopher was, in Salman's own words, 'out of step with orthodoxy'. (Waterstone's Magazine, Autumn 1995 p. 7).

Salman Rushdie's maternal grandparents, Attaullah and Ameer Butt, were Kashmiri Muslims. His father, Anis, is described by Salman as 'a tragic figure, the only son of a rich man, he spent his life losing the money.' (Waterstone's Magazine, p. 7). Salman was brought up in Bombay in an Anglo-phile, Anglo-centric way. Due to his fair complexion he looked white to most of his compatriots. He was, as Phillip Howard, literary editor of The Times says, 'the wrong colour and the wrong religion and the wrong class in the wrong country.' (The Times, 15 February 1989).

When Salman Rushdie was 13, his father sent him to Rugby in England to further his education. Rushdie met discreet English racialism for the first time and realised that he was considered not so much a person as an Indian. When he finished he begged his parents to let him return to India. But he had won an exhibition to Cambridge, and they insisted that he go. Cambridge at least was a success for him. He read history, and with a particular interest he read books that were banned in Islam. In England he had lost his Anglo-Indian snobbery and conservatism and became radical.

After Cambridge he went to Pakistan, whither his parents had removed. He got a job in the country's new television service but ran up against political and religious prejudice due to his outspoken and unorthodox views. This added further to his conflict with, and hatred for Islam which he accredits to his parents; as Rushdie himself says: 'My father was mercifully free of religion. The fact that I was brought up in a religion-free household was my parents' greatest gift to me.' (Waterstone's Magazine. p. 7).

Horrified and disillusioned with Pakistan, he returned to England and scratched a living as an advertising copywriter and in between he started to get on with his 'real writing'. His first marriage was to an English girl called Clarissa Luard, who bore him his only son, Zafar, now in his mid-teens; he later divorced her and married an American novelist Marianne Wiggins from whom he is now separated.

His father died in 1987, escaping knowledge of his son's fate. His mother, Negin, is in her seventies and living in Pakistan. He has three younger sisters, Sameen, Nervid and Nabeelah.

CHAPTER ELEVEN

SALMAN RUSHDIE - THE MAKING OF AN OGRE

Before I look at *The Satanic Verses* objectively, it will be important to briefly glance at Salman Rushdie's previous works and notice a progression of literary style, thought and obsession that propelled into the formation of the infamous novel.

The style, it will be noticed, is that of confusion and disarray; the thoughts are mainly political and religious; and the obsessions are certainly of a sexual nature with coarse usage of foul language. What is apparent from all Rushdie's novels is his wild imagination, which knows no bounds and it is this wild streak that appeals, in a weird sense, to most Western readers who seem to love the extraordinary and the sensational; and if this is interspersed at regular intervals with sex and sensuality, then the Western reader, especially, is hooked. It certainly is a sign of the times that the West, in particular, is obsessed with sex of any kind; the more bizarre, the better.

By reading his novels the reader is left a trail of clues and puzzles that on reflection piece together to form a twisted and perverted mind which crosses the borders of decency, time and time again with unashamed regularity. By reading his novels also, one is easily able to perceive his thoughts about religion, politics, sex, and so on; and what also surfaces is his arrogance and his fears.... The books previous to *The Satanic Verses* are a sort of prior excuse and a prior apology for his later infamous work. This will become more apparent as I briefly discuss the contents of his earlier books in sequence.

GRIMUS

Grimus was Rushdie's first novel which he wrote back in 1975. Who would have known that his very first words published to kick-start his literary career would, in fact, reflect directly on him in a bizarre and eerie manner in a few years time. Note the opening words of the very first chapter of his first ever novel:

'Mr Virgil Jones, a man devoid of friends and with a tongue rather too large for his mouth!'

Mr. Virgil Jones might just as well have been Salman Rushdie himself (in a few years to come).

Grimus was an attempt by Rushdie to create a work of fiction à la Arabian Nights, using the mysticism of the Sufis to try to make his novel a 'stimulating and imaginative one, full of strangely echoing mysteries.'

This mysticism has always fascinated Western readers, and so Rushdie was able to capture their attention at the very beginning and was thus able to make his mark, albeit in a very small way. Nevertheless, *Grimus* went relatively unnoticed - it was an extremely disjointed novel, with no cohesion or congruity; it lacked any real literary style, but what emerged quite clearly was Rushdie's obsession with sex and his crude and coarse style which he employed to win over the Western reader. An example of this:

'I ran around town once with my sex hanging out....I farted into women's faces with my trousers down.'

(p. 239).

On deeper reflection, *The Satanic Verses* seems a glorified revised version of *Grimus*. The similarity is uncanny. The author has gone on a similar mystical voyage crossing the time barriers from present into past, and vice versa in both books. Whereas in *Grimus* it is defined as two distinct parts of the book, inter alia *Times Present* and *Times Past*, in *The Satanic Verses* however, he crosses the time barrier more frequently to add to the confusion. In *Grimus*, Rushdie has disguised the historical figures very cunningly, especially the Islamic ones. In Part Two of the book, in Times Past, the mystical 'K' can certainly be ascribed to the Ka'aba or even, indeed, the Koran. His description of a man called 'Stone' can be none other than Prophet Muhammad(sa). He has ridiculed the Muslims for being blind in their faith and not being able to express freely their own thoughts; for example, in the inside cover of the book it says: 'you will arrive at the town of K where the blinkered and bizarre citizens successfully blind themselves to unacceptable truths about themselves and their island.'

Even the concept of God has been given to ridicule and, in fact, the name Grimus is supposed to be God Himself vis-à-vis The Grim Reaper perhaps. Rushdie has cunningly and mockingly used the Qur'anic style of daring to deny the favours of Allah from Surat Al-Rahman:

'Surely, said Grimus tolerantly. But by shaping you to my grand design I remade you as completely as if you had been unmade clay...... Do you deny that by selecting you as a Recipient I shaped your life thenceforth ?.....Do you deny that by allowing you to wander the world for centuries instead of bringing you here I made you the man you are, chameleon, adaptable, confused ? Do you deny....? Do you deny....? (And then, dropping his voice:) "Which of your Lord's blessings would you deny?"

(p. 293-294).

Note how Rushdie has copied the Qur'anic style in trying to depict a conversation between his 'fictional' God, Grimus and one of his subjects. The relevant verses from Surah Al-Rahman are:

'The Gracious God has taught the Qur'an. He has created man and taught him plain speech... "Which then, of the favours of your Lord will you twain deny, O men and Jinn? He created man from dry ringing clay which is like baked pottery.... Which then, of the favours of your Lord will you twain deny?"

(verses 2-5, 14,15,17).

75

It would be appropriate here to shed some light on the subject matter of Surat Al-Rahman, the 55th chapter of the Holy Qur'an, as some of its verses have been copied almost surreptitiously by Rushdie in almost all his books to continue his derision of Islam and its tenets.

Surat Al-Rahman deals with the basic principles of Islam, i.e. Divine attributes, particularly God's Unity, and with Resurrection and Revelation. It deals with the gifts that God has given to man. The earth with all its treasures, the deep seas and high mountains were all created for his sake. But the whole idea of the 'Grand Design' of God and of His bounties has been dealt a spiteful blow by Rushdie when he writes in his book:

'Flapping Eagle stood in the room he had passed through earlier, the room with veiled objects on podia, wondering what he found alarming about Grimus. He decided it was the childishness underlying his whole so-called Grand Design, the fulfilment of every half-formed whim, and the strangely infantile rituals he devised to amuse him, like this so-called Dance.'

(p. 294)

Rushdie treats the subject most flippantly and he continues this further in the subject relating to Heaven and Hell. In Surat Al-Rahman it is stated that God endowed man with great intellectual and discretionary powers so that by sifting right from wrong he might follow Divine guidance. But the Surah also warns that man, in his conceit and arrogance, seeks to ignore and defy Divine Laws, and consequently brings down upon himself God's punishment.

But, on the other hand, it also says that just as Heavenly Punishment which will be meted out to the guilty and iniquitous will be most grievous and frightful, so would the Divine favours that will be bestowed upon the righteous be beyond measure or count:

'There shall be sent against you a flame of fire, and smoke... And when the heaven is rent asunder, and becomes red like red hide... But for him who fears to stand before his Lord there are

76

two Gardens ... Therein will also be chaste maidens of modest gaze, whom neither man nor Jinn will have touched before them - Which, then, of the favours of your Lord will you twain deny?

(verses 36, 38, 47, 57, 58).

In the same way that the Qur'an deals with the subject of punishment and reward, so Rushdie uses his typically over-imaginative but insensitive style to amuse the reader. The punishment is in the form of:

'Grimus: a baby with a bomb. Or a whole veiled arsenal of bombs. On pedestals.'

(p. 294)

The reward is explained thus:

'The second part of the Dance, Grimus twittered, is a Dance of Veils. In Which Much That Is Wonderful Is Revealed.'

(p. 294)

Rushdie continues this subject in *Midnight's Children* and *Shame*, as discussed later. Other occurrences and similarities can be dug out and there is certainly no denying that the seeds of ridicule and contempt against Islam and its Prophet had been sown in this, his first book. But up until the publication of this book, Salman Rushdie was relatively unknown and had made no impact whatsoever in literary circles or otherwise. Nevertheless, those who saw in him the right ingredients and credentials, were prepared to wait until their prospective accomplice had fully matured with intoxicating qualities.

MIDNIGHT'S CHILDREN

Midnight's Children was Rushdie's second novel, written in 1981, and it brought him a host of literary awards, including the popular and much publicised Booker McConnell Prize for Fiction. It is little short of a miracle that in two easy steps, an author of no previous repute can suddenly become a Booker Prize winner overnight, after having earlier written only one book. But was it indeed, a miracle,

77

or was it more than likely part of the long term plan and ploy of certain powers to heighten the reputation of their secret tool, and then later to let him loose on to the unsuspecting Muslim world?

Midnight's Children is described in the inside jacket cover as a novel about a Saleem Sinai: one of "1,001 children born at that midnight hour, each of them endowed with an extra-ordinary talent - and whose privilege and curse it is to be both masters and victims of their times."

Is it not ironic that the same could be said of Salman Rushdie ? His 'extra-ordinary talent' of the fictitious earned him various accolades of being the 'master' of his profession, among them the Booker Prize for Fiction; but his subsequent work, namely *The Satanic Verses*, became a 'curse' for him, and he did indeed become a 'victim' of the time. It nevertheless has to be stressed that this became a curse for him through his own doing. He was in fact the author of his own destiny. One particular verse of the Holy Qur'an clearly befits the fate of Salman Rushdie:

'So the evil result of what they did befell them, and that which they used to mock at encompassed them.'
(Al-Nahl, Chapter 16, verse 35).

This verse points to the great truth that the punishment of an evil deed is no extraneous thing, but is the natural consequence of the deed itself and is also proportionate to it.

And it is the Majesty of the Supreme Being in fashioning out the fate of an individual by that individual's own contribution to his downfall and in unwittingly predicting his own exact punishment himself. So was the case with Salman Rushdie, who in his earlier books had predicted, unconsciously, his own downfall almost word for word. This will become evident in due course.

Midnight's Children is supposedly a book of fiction (thus the award for Literary Fiction), but Rushdie has used the story of the Midnight's Children against the background of true historical events towards the end of the rule of the British Empire in India and of the Partition and formation of the new Muslim state of Pakistan. Names

78

of true historical figures are also employed, like Ghandi, Jinnah, Mountbatten, Nehru, etc.

Rushdie's thoughts and views are clearly spelt out in this book. He has expressed gratitude to the British a number of times (that's the least he could do since the Arts Council of Great Britain had granted him a literary bursary and financial assistance with all his books!). An example of this appears as an Englishman, William Methwold, a central character in the book, is made to remark condescendingly:

'Hundreds of years of decent government, then suddenly up and off. You'll admit we weren't all bad: built you roads, schools, railway trains, parliamentary system, all worthwhile things. Taj Mahal was falling down until an Englishman bothered to see to it. And now, suddenly, independence.'

(pp. 95-96).

Looking at the book more closely a great deal more can be revealed about Rushdie's childhood, his influences, his base and plebeian desires and his distinct mockery of religion. He gives a feeble excuse as to why he and so many others like him succumbed to Western ways in this statement : 'In India, we've always been vulnerable to Europeans.' (p. 182). A brief insight into his childhood reveals the contempt for religion at a very young age - religion was regarded as a pain and to be taken like a dose of ill-tasting medicine:

'There was not much praying in our family (except at Eid-ul-Fitr, when my father took me to the Friday mosque to celebrate the holiday by tying a handkerchief around my head and pressing my forehead to the ground).'

(p. 178).

Prayer, the most important part of a Muslim's conviction of faith, is given to ridicule and is almost regarded as a penance. Rushdie deeply regretted the Partition, as he had to leave India for Pakistan, due to the fact that he was a Muslim, albeit by name alone, but nevertheless a Muslim:

'I won't deny it: I never forgave Karachi for not being Bombay.'

(p. 299).

He liked the freedom in India where there was no real pressure in having to display Islamic etiquette. But in Pakistan which was formed as a separate country on the very strength of its religion and the freedom to express it, the pressure was much greater to display Islamic characteristics, and he deeply regretted this from very early on. His deep hatred of Pakistan and Islam is made apparent:

'So, from the earliest days of my Pakistani adolescence, I began to learn the secret aromas of the world, the heady but quick-fading perfume of new love, and also the deeper, longer-lasting pungency of hate.'

(p. 298).

Rushdie makes it quite clear, in derision, that he would never fit in 'in the land of the pure' as he 'was forever tainted with Bombayness, his head was full of all sorts of religions apart from Allah's' and that as his 'body was to show a marked preference for the impure', he 'was doomed to be a misfit.' (p. 301).

What he did not realise then was that he would be doomed to be a misfit in almost the whole world in a few years time and that he would be spending his life in hiding. Rushdie also makes a clear differentiation between good and evil and, indubitably, chooses the latter, in arrogant fashion:

'Sacred: purdah-veils, halal meat, muezzin's towers, prayer mats; profane: Western records, pig-meat, alcohol. I understood now why mullahs (sacred) refused to enter aeroplanes (profane) on the night before Id-ul-Fitr, not even willing to enter vehicles whose secret odour was the antithesis of godliness in order to make sure of seeing the new moon I learned the olfactory incompatibility of Islam and socialism....... more and more, however, I became convinced of an ugly truth - namely that the sacred, or good, held little interest for me.'

(p.308).

Rushdie's obsession with sex is also mentioned which started with frequenting prostitutes:

'I explored profanity and lust. (I had money to burn; my father had become generous as well as loving.)'

(p. 309).

But, perhaps the most shocking statement that he makes in this context is the alleged hypocrisy in Muslims when he writes:

'...and no city which locks women away is ever short of whores.'

(p. 309).

His insinuation is that due to the strict laws regarding the purdah (veil) in Islam, there must be an overwhelming demand for whores as the male inhabitants' latent passions have to be satisfied somehow. What an incredulous and incredible claim by the self-confessed master of profanity! Salman Rushdie has furthermore picked out innumerable facets of Islamic beliefs and customs and subjected them to ridicule and contempt. The idea of martyrdom in Islam and its rewards in Paradise also do not escape his venomous pen. He again gives a reference to Surat Al-Rahman:

'Martyrs, Padma! Heroes, bound for the perfumed garden! Where the men would be given four beauteous houris, untouched by man or djinn; and the women, four equally virile males! 'Which of your Lord's blessings would you deny?' What a thing this holy war is, in which with one supreme sacrifice men may atone for all their evils!'

(p. 329).

Note the bitter sarcasm and the gleeful gibe in his writing. The subject of martyrs and righteous people being rewarded with beautiful companions in Heaven as promised in the Holy Qur'an has always been held to ridicule and mockery by Western commentators and Rushdie is no exception as he too joins the band-wagon. But Rushdie, as usual, oversteps the mark by adding his own 'fictional' ingredients. The Qur'anic verses are:

81

'Therein will be maidens, good and beautiful - Fair maidens
with lovely black eyes, well-guarded in pavilions - Which, then,
of the favours of your Lord will you twain deny? Whom neither
man nor Jinn will have touched before them.'

(Surah Al-Rahman, verses 71-75).

Rushdie treats the subject most irreverently by adding, '...and the
women, four equally virile males!' This is certainly meant to titillate
the reader and to take away the sanctity and piety of the righteous
people who are promised noble partners in the Hereafter. But it is
Muhammad(sa) who has been meted out the vilest of abuses. In
fact, Rushdie even has the audacity to make cutting comparisons
with himself, suggesting mockingly that he too has had revelations
in his mind to produce his own works.

Part of a chapter in the book has to be read in its entirety to
perceive the rancour and venom in his pen and where the concept of
revelation is ridiculed to the extreme. I shall just quote a few lines
to present the bitterness to the reader:

'On Mount Sinai, the prophet Musa or Moses heard
disembodied commandments; on Mount Hira, the prophet
Muhammad (also known as Mohammed, Mahomet, the Last-
But-One, and Mahound) spoke to the Archangel (Gabriel or
Jibreel, as you please.)..... but like Musa or Moses, like
Muhammad the Penultimate, I heard voices on a hill.... Gabriel
or Jibreel told Muhammad: 'Recite!' And then began The
Recitation, known in Arabic as Al-Qur'an... That was on Mount
Hira outside Mecca Sharif; on a two-storey hillock opposite
Breach Candy Pools, voices also instructed me to recite.'

(pp. 161-162).

In the same way that Muhammad(sa) went to his wife Khadija to
express his moving experience of his first revelation, so Salman
Rushdie mockingly relates his fictional revelations by rushing to
his parents thus:

'Voices are speaking to me inside my head. I think - Ammi, Abboo, I really think - that Archangels have started to talk to me.'

(p. 162).

However, it is in one reference to Muhammad(sa) that Rushdie's true and dangerous motive surfaces:

'Muhammad (on whose name be peace, let me add; I don't want to offend anyone).'

(p. 161).

Is it not ironic that this is exactly what Rushdie intended to do? He had started to play a dangerous game, which in time was going to become monstrous and ogrous in nature and of which he would no longer have any control. He had made his own proverbial bed in a very early stage of his literary career, and very soon he would be made to lie in it! Due to his conceit and arrogance, one could sense an ominous and foreboding fate awaiting him:

'Muted for an evening and a night and a morning, I struggled, alone, to understand what had happened to me; until at last I saw the shawl of genius fluttering down, like an embroidered butterfly, the mantle of greatness setting upon my shoulders.'

(p. 161).

Through his literary talent, Rushdie thought that he could express whatever views he wished and attribute them to others and thus safeguard his own self; this was a force, a sense of power that he never had before and he seemed to revel in it, as he clearly expresses:

'By sunrise, I had discovered that the voices could be controlled - I was a radio receiver, and could turn the volume down or up; I could select individual voices; I could even, by an effort of will, switch off my newly-discovered inner ear. It was astonishing how soon fear left me.'

(p. 162).

So Salman Rushdie thought that he had discovered a new way to let his true feelings be known and to pass on his message under the guise of fiction, but at the same time exonerating himself beforehand for any recriminations that may ensue. In this way he was able to express his views or the views of those who were paying him (!) on diverse subjects including religion and politics.

In *Midnight's Children*, Rushdie has also tried to convey a political message against the corrupt Pakistani Government. He has tried to expose all that is bad in Pakistani politics to the delight of the West. The political message is, however, dealt with more thoroughly in his next novel *Shame*. As stated while discussing his first novel *Grimus*, his destiny had been pre-ordained and fore-doomed in his own writing. So similarly, in *Midnight's Children*, there is the sense of doom in the final words of the last chapter which could well be a fitting epitaph for the author:

'Yes, they will trample me underfoot,....reducing me to specks of voiceless dust,... because it is the privilege and the curse of midnight's children to be both masters and victims of their times, to forsake privacy and be sucked into the annihilating whirlpool of the multitudes, and to be unable to live or die in peace.'

(p. 446).

How chillingly this has proved to be the case of Salman Rushdie. It was almost as if he had dug his own grave.

This comparable study of Rushdie's work can easily lead a reader to ascertain for himself the long-term plan and ploy to present Rushdie as an author of great talent and repute in granting him the ultimate recognition by bestowing endless literary awards upon him, including the grandest of them all, the Booker Prize for Literature for Fiction. But when you look at his work more closely, you cannot help but wonder who the books were aimed at. Surely it could not be for the benefit of the Western reader, as the books are interspersed with so many Hindi and Urdu words that someone without any basic knowledge of these languages would struggle to comprehend its relevance, e.g. 'sabkuch ticktack hai, Gai-wallah, cooch naheen', etc. Almost every other page is littered with Hindi words that would certainly be off-putting for those who would have to revert to a dictionary all the time and would progress through the novel laboriously.

Or could it be that the books were written for the benefit of those Europeans who ruled in India and their families who had a more than average knowledge of the Asian languages? Even so, the range of readership must have been extremely limited and could not have warranted Salman Rushdie becoming a Booker Prize winner.

Surely, all the signs point to a deliberate plan to build the reputation of Rushdie by any means and to use him as a guinea-pig. He was probably aware of that fact, but it did not seem to matter to him, as long as he was being bestowed worldly honours and promised untold riches. And Rushdie certainly hints at the fact that there was worse still to come:

> 'Archangels no longer speak to mortals....the voices in my head far outnumbered the ranks of the angels.... My voices, far from being sacred, turned out to be as profane, and as multitudinous, as dust...... But I ask for patience - wait..... Don't write me off too easily.'
>
> (p. 166).

SHAME

Rushdie's third novel, published in 1983, had an appropriate name - it hinted at a characteristic that he certainly lacked. When we now read Rushdie's earlier novels, after witnessing the infamous debacle of *The Satanic Verses*, we cannot help but notice how frequently he has put his foot in his mouth and how his work has reverberated on him. A classic example of this is found in page 39:

> 'No matter how determinedly one flees a country, one is obliged to take along some hand-luggage; and can it be doubted that Omar Khayyam.... having been barred from feeling shame.. at an early age, continued to be affected by that remarkable ban throughout his later years.'

How the predicament of Omar Khayyam (the central figure in the novel) has rebounded on Rushdie himself. Salman Rushdie has in fact been fleeing from one country to another like a frightened jack-ass, and his state is such that he still expresses no shame at all at what he has done. His assault on all things Islamic is continued in this novel also. For example, even the Muslim form of worship is ridiculed:

'Muhammad Ibadalla, who bore upon his forehead the 'gatta' or permanent bruise which revealed him to be a religious fanatic who pressed brow to prayer-mat on at least five occasions per diem, and probably at the sixth, optional time as well.'

(p. 41-42).

To pray five times a day is the minimal requirement for a Muslim, and is the normal practice of most ordinary Muslims, but Rushdie regards this as being the practice of a religious fanatic. This clearly shows how alienated Rushdie is from Islam and also how contemptuously he regards it. His hatred of Pakistan resurfaces when he gleefully admits that as *Shame* is a 'fictional' novel, he need not write the truth of the 'goings on' in the politics and the general way of life in Pakistan. He stupidly tries to disguise his motives by pre-supposing the obvious. As he writes, (pp. 69-70):

'But suppose this were a realistic novel! Just think what else I might have put in. The business, for instance, of the illegal installation, by the richest inhabitants of 'Defence', of covert, subterranean water pumps that steal water from their neighbours' mains....And would I also have to describe the Sind Club in Karachi, where there is still a sign reading 'Women and Dogs Not Allowed Beyond This Point'?.... the execution of Mr Zulfikar Ali Bhutto..... or about anti-Semitism.... or about smuggling, the boom in heroin exports, military dictators, venal civilians, corrupt civil servants, bought judges.'

and he sarcastically ends by saying:

'Imagine my difficulties!'

Rushdie has tried to be smug in clearly and unequivocally expressing all his anger and anti-Pakistani thoughts by saying that he could not mention them because 'this is not a realistic novel'. He has openly referred to the corruption in Pakistan at all levels and has insinuated at the supposed third-class status of women in society by equating them to dogs. Perhaps the most poignant and acrid statement is made in the very next two paragraphs which have an eerie premonition of events and circumstances that were to befall him, keeping in mind that this novel was written in 1983, some five years prior to *The Satanic Verses*. Notice how each word and sentence was to play a fateful and ominous part and was to turn his life upside-down:

'By now, if I had been writing a book of this nature, it would have done me no good to protest that I am writing universally, not only about Pakistan. The book would have been banned, dumped in the rubbish bin, burned. All that effort for nothing! Realism can break a writer's heart. Fortunately, however, I am only telling a sort of modern fairy-tale, so that's all right; nobody need get upset, or take anything I say too seriously. No drastic action need be taken, either. What a relief!'

(p. 70).

As this book had received scant publicity, Rushdie's views and observations had gone relatively unnoticed. But those that saw the author as a tool who fulfilled all the requirements for their nefarious plans must have been wringing their hands in sheer delight, as they were presented with an opportunity they could not afford to let go. The ominous signs, nevertheless, were already there in Rushdie's own writings and it would not be too long before he would be using the same arguments to try to find loopholes to escape through, but sadly for him there would be no reprieve and it would certainly not provide any 'relief' for him - in fact, it would be quite the opposite; his very life would be in danger and he would never have guessed that all the arguments he had used in a mocking and foolhardy manner would be his very life-line. Rushdie's arrogance and sense of shame at being associated with ordinary Pakistani Muslims is seen clearly

87

while he writes about the villagers:

> 'O God, Ignoramuses from somewhere. Backward types, village idiots, unsophisticated completely, and I am stuck with them.'

(p. 74)

His taunts at Islamic beliefs and Qur'anic verses are also expressed and he quotes from Surah Al-Rahman yet again. (Perhaps this is the only part he knows !)

While writing about the Indo-Pakistan war on the Kashmir frontier, he writes that:

> 'There were, inevitably, deaths; but the organisers of the war had catered for these as well. Those who fell in battle were flown directly, first class, to the perfumed gardens of Paradise, to be waited on for all eternity by four gorgeous Houris, untouched by man or djinn. "Which of your Lord's blessings", the Qur'an inquires, "would you deny?"'

(p. 77).

This is an exact replica of the subject that Rushdie has mocked in his previous book *Midnight's Children*, and which bears an uncanny similarity to the defamatory language used by earlier critics of Islam, like Peter the Venerable and Thomas Aquinas discussed earlier. Rushdie, in all his books, and especially, in *Shame*, has related mundane and everyday instances of normal life in Pakistan and has deliberately picked out the warts in that society and highlighted them in trying to portray a sense of hypocrisy, corruption, bigotry and all things nasty in the Muslim state of Pakistan. He has included politicians, singers, film stars, sportsmen, religious leaders, the Media and even ordinary villagers. Rushdie has acted almost like a spy for the West, to expose the ills of Pakistan's Muslim society in ensanguined detail, without any sense of shame.

In his discourse about Pakistani politics it is quite clear that he favoured Zulfikar Ali Bhutto, as Bhutto himself was a puppet of the West. Bhutto, and his children also, had been educated in Britain and were lovers of all things Western. What is also clear is Rushdie's

88

contempt for Zia-ul-Haq and his 'Islamization' of Pakistan.

It has become quite apparent that Rushdie stands for everything un-Islamic, so it was natural for him to scorn scathingly Zia's Islamic rule of Government and Zia's ideals. Rushdie also relates Bhutto's execution by Zia-ul-Haq using fictional characters. (pp. 230-231). Even Benazir Bhutto's plight is mentioned sympathetically, and her character is also disguised using a fictional name.

The fictional characters used, however, do not for a moment disguise the real political message that Rushdie wishes to convey. He was totally against the Zia regime in every way, and has openly expressed favouritism for the Pakistan People's Party of which Zulfikar Bhutto was once the leader. He has used the character of General Raza to represent Zia and has deliberately highlighted Zia's crude tactics so that Rushdie could portray Islam in a barbaric and impure light. For example:

'On the Prophet's birthday Raza arranged for every mosque in the country to sound a siren at nine a.m. and anybody who forgot to stop and pray when he heard the howling was instantly carted off to jail..... He announced that God and socialism were incompatible, so that the doctrine of Islamic Socialism on which the Popular Front has based its appeal was the worst kind of blasphemy imaginable.... that men would spit at women in the street if they went about their business with their midriffs showing; and that a person could be strangled for smoking a cigarette during the month of fasting.'

(pp. 247-248).

A whole chapter entitled, 'Beauty and the Beast', (pp. 146-173) is devoted to humiliating Pakistan in its treatment of women. The idea of arranged marriages is disdainfully dealt with and the supposed maltreatment of women by Muslim men is highlighted. The notion of Muslim women being in chains is highlighted more and more to portray Pakistan as an uncultured and savage country controlled by its religious beliefs. As Rushdie writes:

'It is commonly and, I believe, accurately said of Pakistan that her women are much more impressive than her men... their chains, nevertheless, are no fictions. They exist. And they are getting heavier.'

(p. 173).

The Western scholars' theories on fundamentalist Islam are also exposed in Rushdie's writing and the subject is dealt equal disdain. He talks of the Islamic state of Pakistan as 'hapless' due to its mythological ideas regarding its religion, which he explains is the reason for its apparent decline in popularity:

'Few mythologies survive close examination, however. And they can become very unpopular indeed if they're rammed down people's throats. What happens if one is force-fed such outsize, indigestible meals? - One gets sick. One rejects their nourishment. Reader: one pukes. So-called Islamic 'fundamentalism' does not spring, in Pakistan, from the people. It is imposed on them from above... This is how religions shore up dictators; by encircling them with words of power, words which the people are reluctant to see discredited, disenfranchised, mocked... In the end you get sick of it, you lose faith in the faith.'

(p. 251).

And just as in his previous books, the end of *Shame* also describes, in his own words, the pending doom that is destined for him. It would certainly not be too long before his proverbial high-flying bubble would burst : the Power of the Beast of shame cannot be held for long within any one frame of flesh and blood, because it grows, it feeds and swells, until the vessel bursts. (p. 286)

It seemed now after the publication of *Shame*, that Salman Rushdie was 'ripe for the killing'. He was now in a state of total insobriety, intoxicated with the lure of riches and fame at any cost, with no 'shame' whatsoever. He had now truly acquired Mephisthophelean qualities. He had sold himself lock, stock and barrel and was very much in the stranglehold of his manipulators.

90

There was a lull of almost five years before Salman Rushdie was unleashed onto the world scene with one of the most infamous pieces of literary work in history. And perhaps, one of his wishes was granted that his would become a household name, but all for the wrong reasons.

THE SATANIC VERSES

It has been strongly argued by Salman Rushdie and his supporters that *The Satanic Verses* was a fictitious novel and that no one had the right to restrict his imagination. On examining the novel in greater detail, the reader can be left in no doubt that many of the characters depicted are anything but imaginary.

Rushdie continues to stress that the story he has concocted in the novel is entirely imaginary in that it has no bearing on reality whatsoever. However, whilst the story may be unreal and indeed imaginary, the tale is woven around very real and well-known people. Usually, in any work of fiction, there is a disclaimer to the effect that 'all the events and characters in the book are entirely fictitious, and are not intended to represent any actual event or real person, either living or dead.' Interestingly enough Rushdie makes no such declaration in his novel.

By way of example I shall quote just a few extracts from the novel to let the reader decide for himself the untenable and flimsy defence of the author. Perhaps, to the Western readers, due to their lack of knowledge of Islamic history and unfamiliarity with the names of Prophet Muhammad's companions, the connotations and inferences implied by some of the passages go unnoticed and they would thus regard the novel as fictitious, but to the thousands of millions of Muslims all around the globe who hold the holy personages of Islam in the greatest of reverence, this was nothing more than a deliberate and concerted effort to injure their feelings for no apparent reason.

It is not my intention to relate all the blasphemous language in the book, nor to relate all the hurtful inferences to the noble

91

personages of Islam, for this would run into several hundreds of pages. Instead I will only relate a few examples to illustrate the author's mendacious claim and insistence that this is a work of fiction. What will also surface is the author's hatred of everything Islamic.

The Holy Qur'an was revealed to Prophet Muhammad(sa) through the Archangel Gabriel. In Urdu an angel is called a 'farishta'. One of the central characters in the novel is 'Gibreel Farishta', who throughout has been referred to as a sex-starved half-god, half-human, on the loose, who indulges in all sorts of vices including adultery, incest and eating of pork just to prove that God is no longer omnipotent. (pp. 25-30).

Is the use of a revered figure in Islamic belief in such ignominious terms a necessary addition to a supposedly 'fictitious' novel? Or is the author so oblivious to the sensitive feelings of millions of Muslims all around the world? Mecca, which is regarded as the most sacred city in Islam, is called the 'city of Jahlia', meaning a city of ignorance. (p. 95).

Prophet Abraham(as) is called a 'bastard' (p. 95) and the companions of the Holy Prophet(sa) are also spared no poison from his pen. Salman Farsi is called amongst other names 'some sort of bum', Bilal is called an 'enormous black monster'; these two noble companions plus another one called Khalid are regarded as 'riff-raff, trinity of scum, idlers' and 'those goons those f...ing clowns'. (pp. 101-102). The Prophet's uncle Hamza is also insulted (p. 104).

Can it be purely coincidental that the names of so many 'fictional' characters in the book resemble those of the companions of the Holy Prophet(sa) of Islam, or was the real aim to injure and hurt the feelings of Muslims all over the world ? Was it also coincidental that the brothel named 'Hijab', which supposedly existed at the time of the Holy Prophet(sa), was full of whores who are given names which are the same as the names of the noble wives of the Holy Prophet(sa)?

It is a well-known fact, and a non-practising Muslim like Rushdie would also be aware of this, that the wives of the Holy Prophet(sa) had a revered status as 'the Mothers of the Faithful', and this deliberate comparison was surely to incite passionate rage amongst the Muslims who would treat this as more insulting to them than if their own wives and mothers were insulted.

Perhaps Rushdie in his naivety and stupidity thought that under the guise of fiction he could get away with anything! And he has stretched this pretence to the limit, so much so that even his own supporters must have felt embarrassed about his devious scheme.

Rushdie's hatred of Islam continues in this novel and he tauntingly jibes at everything Islamic, no matter how trivial. For example, he insinuates that a Muslim's life is governed by all sorts of rules and he is thus not free to express his own self:

'The faithful lived by lawlessness, but in those years Mahound ... became obsessed by law..... rules, rules, rules... rules about every damn thing, if a man farts let him turn his face to the wind, a rule about which hand to use for the purpose of cleaning one's behind. It was as if no aspect of human existence was to be left unregulated, free. The revelation - the recitation - told the faithful how much to eat, how deeply they should sleep, and which sexual positions had received divine sanction...'

(pp. 364-5).

Rushdie also ridicules the Islamic form of ablution and prayers:

'Ablutions, always ablutions, the legs up to the knees, the arms down to the elbows, the head down to the neck. Dry-torsoed, wet-limbed and damp-headed, what eccentrics they look! Splish, splosh, washing and praying. On their knees, pushing arms, legs, heads back into the ubiquitous sand, and then beginning again the cycle of water and prayer.'

(p. 104).

Rushdie has clearly ridiculed the laws of Sharia in Islam by using foul language as he did in *Midnight's Children*. But in *Satanic Verses* he has gone at length on this subject and throughout the book he continually refers to the restrictive nature of the Islamic law compared to the free-for-all Western society of which he is a proud member. There is absolutely nothing fictitious about which religion he is ridiculing, but in fact it is in direct keeping with the anti-Islamic theme that is clearly apparent, not only in this book, but in all his books.

Any ordinary Muslim would have been incensed by the contents discussed so far in this book, but if this was not enough, Salman Rushdie had saved the deadliest poison for the Holy Prophet of Islam(sa). He has used the name 'Mahound' to describe Muhammad(sa). This was in accordance with the medieval propaganda through the Crusades, which had built up a conception of Muhammad(sa) as 'the great enemy' to Christendom who was transformed into Mahound, the prince of darkness. In *Midnight's Children* he clearly states, 'The prophet Muhammed (also known as...Mahound),' (p. 161).

It has been painful enough to labour through the novel and to try to keep a sound frame of mind at the calumnious nature and vindictive language aimed at the nobler than noble character of the Holy Prophet(sa); and I would certainly not like to impose it upon anyone; even so, were I to give examples it would necessitate quoting almost the entire book.

A lot has already been written on this subject by numerous Muslim scholars; suffice it to say that this book is littered with obscenities against Prophet Muhammad(sa). Though the attacks on his noble character resemble those of earlier orientalists, Rushdie has stooped the lowest by using the foulest and most vindictive language imaginable. And to bestow literary awards on the author for this sort of work is like twisting the knife that is already deeply entrenched in the back of Muslims.

CHAPTER TWELVE

THE FICTION OF THE SATANIC VERSES

I will now, however, look at the subject of the satanic verses; how it has been suggested by almost all the Western orientalists that Muhammad(sa) was supposedly prone to ordinary human frailties and that on some occasions satanic influences entered his mind which were then transmitted into some verses of the Holy Qur'an.

The main point of contention relates to a few verses from Surah Al-Najm, the 53rd Chapter of the Holy Qur'an. The verses in question are numbers 20 and 21:

Now tell me about Lat and Uzza;
And Manat, the third one, another goddess.

Some prejudiced critics of the Holy Prophet(sa) have woven quite a fantastic story of his having once fallen a victim to the machinations of Satan.

It is stated that one day at Mecca, when the Holy Prophet(sa) recited this Surah before a mixed assembly of Muslims and disbelievers and during the recitation he came to these verses, Satan contrived to put in his mouth the words:

'these are exalted goddesses and their intercession is hoped for.'

(Zurqani).

They talk of the 'lapse of Muhammad' or his 'compromise with idolatry' and seem to rely for this entirely baseless story upon Waqidi, the renowned inveterate liar and fabricator of reports, and on Tabari, who is generally regarded as a credulous and indiscriminate narrator of events. These gentlemen have the audacity to attribute this blasphemous utterance to that great iconoclast (the Holy Prophet(sa)) whose entire life was spent in denouncing and condemning idolatry and who carried out his noble mission with unremitting vigour and fearless devotion, spurning all offers of compromise with idol-worship, and whom blandishments, bribes, cajolery or intimidation failed to move an inch from his set purpose, and to whose unshakeable firmness against idolatry the Almighty Himself has borne testimony (Ch. 18, v. 7).

Moreover, the whole context belies this baseless assertion. Not only the verses that follow, but the entire Surah contains an unsparing condemnation of idolatry and an uncompromising insistence on Divine Unity. It is strange that this patent fact should have escaped the notice of the Holy Prophet's critics and carpers.

Historical data too lend no support whatever to this so-called 'lapse'. The story has been rejected as completely unreliable by all the learned Commentators of the Qur'an, Ibn Kathir and Razi among them. The renowned leaders of Muslim religious thought, well-versed in the science of Hadith (the sayings of the Holy Prophet(sa)), have regarded it as pure invention. No trace of this story is to be found in the Six Reliable Collections of Hadith. Imam Bhukari, whose collection, the 'Sahih Bukhari', is regarded by Muslim scholars as the most reliable book of Hadith, and who himself was a contemporary of Waqidi to whom goes the unenviable credit of forging and reporting this story, makes no mention of it, nor does the great historian, Ibn Ishaq, who was born more than 40 years before him.

96

But to the hardened critics and enemies of Islam this presented an opportunity for them to use their guile and deceit to the full and thus continue their vindictive assault on the Founder of Islam. The critics have always been on the look-out to discover a lapse on the part of the Holy Prophet(sa) and when they can find none, they invent one and impute it to him, like the one that relates to the subject in hand. For some reason this certain lie appealed to many of the orientalists who have used it in their respective books in almost carbon-copy fashion.

Note the reference to this subject by just some of these Western writers and how similar they are in dealing with it and also the way that Rushdie imputes the satanic thoughts to the Holy Prophet(sa).

MAXIME RODINSON

Let us first examine how Rodinson relates the above-mentioned incident. In his book *Mohammed*, Rodinson describes the incident as 'reasonably true because the makers of Muslim tradition would never have invented a story with such damaging implications for the revelation as a whole.' (p. 106) He quotes Tabari, the renowned fabricator of events:

'When the Messenger of God saw his people draw away from him, it gave him great pain to see what a distance separated them from the word of Allah which he brought to them. Then he longed in his heart to receive a word from Allah which would bring him closer to his people..... It was then that Allah revealed to him the 'surah' of the Star....'

When he came to the verse:
'Have you considered Allat and al-'Uzza
And Manat, the third, the other?...' (Koran liii, 19-20)

'the demon put upon his tongue what he had been saying to himself and would have liked to hand on to his people:'

'They are the Exalted Birds
And their intercession is desired indeed.'

'It was only later that the archangel revealed to Muhammad
that he had been deceived by the Devil - although, he added as
consolation, that was no wonder because the earlier prophets
had experienced similar difficulties and for the same reasons.

The additional verses were taken out and replaced by others
rejecting the cult of the 'three great aquatic birds'.... Obviously
(Tabari's account as good as says so in fairly clear words)
Muhammad's unconscious had suggested to him a formula which
provided a practical road to unanimity.'

(pp. 106-7).

Maxime Rodinson has obviously copied almost word for word the
fantastic story concocted by earlier orientalists and has also hinted
at the ordinary human frailties of Muhammad(sa) which he equates
to other prophets before him.

DR. NAZIR ALI

Dr. Ali, the first Asian Diocese Bishop in England, has also used
the same line in falsely attributing satanic thoughts to Prophet
Muhammad(sa) in his book *Islam, A Christian Perspective* Dr. Ali
hints at the assumption that Muhammad(sa) made compromises in
order that his message would be accepted by the local inhabitants:

'In the end one may have to conclude that although
Muhammad desired continuity with the Judaeo-Christian
tradition, he desired continuity with traditional Arab religion
and culture as well (This may account for his original acceptance
of the goddesses Lat, Manat and 'Uzza as intercessors with Allah.
He said later that this verse had been inspired by Satan, and
changed it!)'

(pp. 24-25).

MONTGOMERY WATT

Though Watt dispels the view that Muhammad(sa) forged the Qur'an, he nevertheless casts doubt on some of the verses which he believes have been abrogated to suit the situation. For example, in *Muhammad at Medina*, he writes of the so-called 'revised' passages:

'The revision, if it may be so called, consists in the addition or omission of words, phrases, and longer passages. Muhammad may be presumed to have regarded these changes as emendations communicated to him by God to meet fresh circumstances. A certain amount of revision is admitted by Muslim orthodoxy in its doctrine that some verses have been abrogated.'

(p 326).

Montgomery Watt has been one of the most ardent critics of the Holy Prophet(sa), and Watt's dubious style has always left a bitter after-taste in the mouth. Note the conniving way that he uses Qur'anic and historical data out of context to portray a less-than-perfect image of the character of the Holy Prophet(sa) in another of his books, *Islamic Fundamentalism and Modernity*:

'Muhammad was held to be perfect in every way, and never to have been a pagan, despite the fact that the Qur'an (93.7) speaks of him as 'erring' (dall), and other sources report that he had sacrificed to the local deities. This idealisation of Muhammad leads modern Muslims to reject the story of the 'satanic verses' although it is accepted by the eminent historian and exegete at-Tabari and has some support from a verse in the Qur'an (22.52). The story is that, on one occasion, while Muhammad was hoping that he might receive a revelation which would bring over to his side the leaders of Quraysh hostile to him, Satan inserted verses into the revelation permitting intercession to three local goddesses. Muhammad thought these verses were part of the genuine revelation, proclaimed them publicly, and was joined by the Meccan leaders in an act of Islamic worship. Later he realised that he had been mistaken

99

about these verses and proclaimed a revised form, not allowing intercession, and thus caused the Meccans to turn away from him.'

(pp. 17/18).

Watt repeats this theme in greater detail in another of his books *Muslim-Christian Encounters*:

'On one occasion, as Muhammad was sitting with pagan merchants and hoping he might have a revelation which would win them over, he began to receive a revelation with the words:

"Have you considered al-Lat and al-'Uzza, and Manat, the third, the other?"

(53:19f)

Next came two (or in some versions three) verses allowing a worshiper to ask these pagan goddesses to intercede on his behalf with Allah, the high god... Later, however, he realised that the second group of verses had been intruded by Satan and were not genuine.'

(p. 114).

To make this claim more forceful, Watt adds that 'this story comes from an impeccable Muslim source' (p. 114) and that 'it is unthinkable that any Muslim would have invented such a story, or that at-Tabari, who was a careful scholar, would have accepted it from a dubious source.' (p. 115).

Montgomery Watt uses the same argument in almost all his books; it is as if this particular incident carries the most weight in attributing moral lapses on the part of the Holy Prophet(sa) thus tainting his 'perfect' image that the Muslims boast about. It is no wonder then that most western writers revert to this episode time and time again; and it is equally not surprising when this subject was chosen as the main title for a novel.

KAREN ARMSTRONG

In her book, *Muhammad, A Western Attempt To Understand Islam*, Karen Armstrong devotes a whole chapter to the subject of 'The. Satanic Verses' and, in my view, gives a more balanced and neutral argument by quoting the different versions of the story and by expressing doubts about some of the sources and letting the readers decide for themselves the authenticity of the whole episode.

While discussing this episode, Armstrong observes that 'this story is in conflict with other traditions and with the Qur'an itself.' She goes on to remind us 'that a Muslim historian like Tabari does not necessarily endorse all the traditions he records; he expects the reader to compare them with others and to make up his or her own mind about their validity.' (p. 113).

Armstrong also discloses that Tabari has more than one version of the story: 'In his history Tabari also preserves a tradition which gives a very different version of the story.' (p . 113). This clearly shows up Tabari's source and narrations to be totally unreliable.

In another part of the chapter Karen Armstrong gives the argument of the majority of the Muslims in refuting this story and also sincerely talks of the opportunity that it afforded the enemies of Islam to take advantage of:

'We have to be clear here that many Muslims believe this story to be apocryphal. They point out that there is no clear reference to it in the Qur'an... nor in the great collections of traditions (ahadith) about Muhammad... by Bukhari and Muslim. Muslims do not reject traditions simply because they could be interpreted critically, but because they are insufficiently attested. Western enemies of 'Islam', however, have seized upon it to illustrate Muhammad's manifest insincerity: how could a man who changed the divine Word to suit himself be a true prophet? Surely any genuine prophet would be able to distinguish between a divine and a satanic inspiration? Would a man of God tamper with his revelation merely to attract more converts?'

(p. 109).

And this is exactly the argument that the 'Western enemies of Islam' have employed to cast doubts and aspersions on the authenticity of the verses in question and the faith and character of the Holy Prophet(sa).

CHAPTER THIRTEEN

RUSHDIE'S TREATMENT
OF THE SATANIC VERSES

Rushdie has obviously made continued reference to the 'satanic verses' throughout his infamous book and although he has tried to treat the subject as frivolously and as facetiously as possible, it cannot hide the venom and the contempt behind it all. Note also the way that Rushdie has used the concocted stories of some of the Western writers on this subject and tried to dress it in the guise of fiction:

> 'Nearing him, she halted, and recited in her terrible voice of sulphur and hellfire: 'Have you heard of Lat, and Manat, and Uzza, the Third, the Other? They are the Exalted Birds'... But Khalid interrupted her, saying, 'Uzza, those are the Devil's verses, and you the Devil's daughter, a creature not to be worshipped, but denied.' So he drew his sword and cut her down.'
>
> (p. 373).

Rushdie's continual transition in the book from the past to the present and vice-versa has been designed to leave the reader in confusion and doubt. By using the modern-day foul language and relating the ills of modern-day society, he insinuates that at the time of the Holy Prophet(sa) also there must have been weaknesses on the part of not only his Companions but on the part of the Holy Prophet(sa) himself. For example, in the writing down of the Holy Qur'an by

the scribes, Rushdie clearly hints at the assumption that
Muhammad(sa) sometimes used to overlook some of the minor
mistakes of the scribes. Writing about Salman Farsi, Rushdie writes:

> '...when he sat at the Prophet's feet, writing down rules rules,
> rules, he began, surreptitiously, to change things. 'Little things
> at first. If Mahound recited a verse in which God was described
> as 'all-hearing, all knowing', I would write, 'all-knowing, all-
> wise'. Here's the point: Mahound did not notice the alterations.
> So there I was, actually writing the Book, or re-writing, anyway,
> polluting the word of God with my own profane language.'
>
> (p. 367).

This has been the theme throughout the book; but the *coup-de-grace*
has been the filthy language accompanying the story and the spiteful
and mordacious calumnies levelled at the Holy Prophet(sa), his noble
wives and his Companions. He has related all the famous Islamic
historical events, real names and real circumstances, and he has the
audacity to pass it all off as fiction. Just by way of example I shall
quote only a few passages:

> 'His name: a dream-name....pronounced correctly, it means
> he-for-whom-thanks-should-be-given, but he won't answer to
> that here.... Here he is neither Mahomet nor MoeHammered;
> has adopted, instead, the demon-tag the farangis hung around
> his neck.... our mountain-climbing, prophet-motivated solitary
> is to be the medieval baby-frightener, the Devil's synonym:
> Mahound.'
>
> (p. 93).

> 'Mahound's anguish is awful. He asks: is it possible that
> they are angels? Lat, Manat, Uzza...can I call them angelic? Are
> these the daughters of God?.... Is Allah so unbending that he
> will not embrace three more to save the human race?'
>
> (p. 111).

> 'He (Mahound) stands in front of the statues of the Three
> and announces the abrogation of the verses which Shaitan
> whispered in his ear. These verses are banished from the true

104

recitation, al-Qur'an. New verses are thundered in their place. 'Shall He have daughters and you sons?' Mahound recites. 'That would be a fine division!'

(p. 124)

'He turned to face Ayesha. 'There is no God,' he said firmly. 'There is no God but God, and Muhammad is His Prophet,' she replied.'

(p. 239).

The Battle of the Ditch is also mentioned:

'Salman had persuaded the Prophet to have a huge trench dug all the way around the unwalled oasis settlement... A ditch: with sharpened stakes at the bottom. When the Jahilians saw this foul piece of unsportsman-like hole-digging their sense of chivalry and honour obliged them to behave as if the ditch had not been dug, and to ride their horses at it, full-tilt.... trust an immigrant not to play the game.'

(p. 365).

SALMAN FARSI

It is worth mentioning here who Salman Farsi really was as this may help explain why he too became a target of Rushdie's poisoned pen. Salman Farsi was born of Persian Zoroastrian parents in the village of Jayy near Isfahan. After converting to Christianity he travelled to Syria whilst still young. There he became a companion of a saintly bishop who, on his deathbed, advised Salman to go to the Bishop of Mosul, who was old but was the best man he knew. Salman set off for the north of Iraq, a journey which was to be the beginning of a series of attachments to early Christian sages until the last of these sages, also on his deathbed, told Salman that the time of the appearance of a prophet was now at hand:

'He will be sent with the religion of Abraham and will come forth in Arabia where he will emigrate from his home to a place between two lava tracts, a country of palms. His signs are manifest: he will eat of a gift but not if given as alms; and

105

between his shoulders is the seal of the prophecy.'

Salman made up his mind to find this prophet and paid a party of merchants of the Kalb tribe to take him with them to Arabia. However upon reaching Wadi al-Qura near the Gulf of Aqabah at the north of the Red Sea, they sold him as a slave to a Jew. The sight of palms in Wadi al-Qura made him wonder whether this could be the township he was seeking, but he had his doubts. The Jew sold him to a cousin of his of the Bani Quraiza tribe in Medina. Salman's new owner had another cousin who lived in Quba, and on arrival of the Prophet this Jew of Quba set off for Medina with the news.

Salman was working at the top of a tree while his slave master was sitting under its shade. When Salman heard the Jew from Quba relate to his cousin that a man claiming to be a prophet had arrived there, he was certain that his hopes had been realised. Such was the impact of this news that his body began to tremble and he almost fell out of the tree. That evening he slipped away from his slave master and went to Quba. There he found the Prophet(sa) sitting with his Companions. Salman approached him and offered him some food specifying that he gave it as alms. The Prophet(sa) told the others to partake of the food but did not eat any himself. Though he had been convinced of the truth of the Prophet as soon as he had laid his eyes on him, this abstinence of the Holy Prophet(sa) convinced him even more. His second meeting with the Prophet(sa) took place at the funeral of As'ad. Salman described this meeting years later to his son Abbas:

'I went to the Messenger of God when he was in Baqi al Ghrqad (Cemetery at the south east end of Medina) whither he had followed the bier of one of his Companions.' {While the Prophet was sitting there with some of his companions after the burial} 'I greeted him and then circled round behind him in the hope that I might be able to look upon the Seal. And he knew what I desired, so he grasped his cloak and threw it off his back, and I beheld the Seal of the Prophecy even as my Master

106

described it unto me. I stooped over it and kissed it and wept. Then the Messenger of God bade me come round and I went and sat in front of him and told him my story and he was glad that his companions should hear it. Then I entered Islam.' (Extracts from *Mohammad* by Martin Lings).

Salman Farsi's noble character is evident in his mannerisms and his perception of the truth, but even such pious personalities did not deter Rushdie in his slander. In fact what is apparent in Rushdie's writings is his complete disregard for the sentiments of all Muslims, irrespective of their particular sect. His superficial veil of fiction, which he uses to hide his ulterior motives, is transparent beyond belief. Whilst he may have written a whole book entitled 'Shame', it is evidently one characteristic that he does not possess. Not satisfied with reviling the Holy Prophet(sa) of Islam, Rushdie sets upon the esteemed Companions as well, adding insult to injury. Even with those Companions who remain honoured and cherished by all the branches of Islam, the Companions whose life examples generate respect and admiration, are not spared. Such a Companion was Salman Farsi - a person whose dedication to Islam and loyalty is acknowledged by the whole of the Muslim world. His knowledge and sincerity was respected by the Holy Prophet(sa) himself.

One such incident illustrates this well and this was also perhaps Salman Farsi's most famous contribution in the annals of Islam. And this interestingly enough is also the incident that Rushdie relates with his customary derision in *The Satanic Verses* (p.365). It was a time when the Muslims had been forced to migrate from Mecca to Yathrab - a town approximately 250 miles north of Mecca. (Yathrab later became known as Medina-tun-nabi, or Medina for short). At the time of the migration of the Holy Prophet(sa), there were a number of local people who had already embraced Islam; they were known as the Ansar. The Muslims who migrated to Medina either with the Holy Prophet(sa) or afterwards, were known as the Emigrants. The Muslims remained there for many years, constantly under the threat of attack from the tribe of Quraish - who were extending their influence over other local tribes. At one time the Quraish had gathered over 10 000 warriors to invade Medina and wipe out Islam once and for all.

The Muslims were far fewer both in number and armoury. When the Holy Prophet(sa) learned of the imminent attack he summoned his Companions for consultation - Salman Farsi was one of them. He suggested that the Muslims could secure themselves by digging a wide trench around the part of Medina which was vulnerable. The Holy Prophet(sa) accepted his suggestion and orders were given to dig the trench - the work was split between the Ansar and the Emigrants, upon which a question arose as to which party Salman Farsi should assist. This was put to the Holy Prophet(sa), who observed with a smile:

'Salman is neither Emigrant nor Ansar; he is a member of my family and is one of us.'

From that time onwards Salman was always known as a member of the Holy Prophet's family. This clearly shows the lofty position of Salman Farsi in the history of Islam, yet in Rushdie's mind this doesn't have the slightest effect, for it is the very pearls of Islam that he seeks to defile. The worst treatment is meted out to the Holy Prophet(sa) himself and his wives. Islamic teachings are ridiculed, and Islamic personalities are trashed. In his crusade for freedom of expression, Rushdie has left common courtesy by the wayside, showing not even the slightest concern for the feelings of his fellow beings.

FURTHER ALLEGATIONS AGAINST THE PROPHET

Going back to *The Satanic Verses*, matters relating to polygamy and the alleged licentiousness of the Holy Prophet(sa) have also been treated with the most potent poison:

'In spite of the ditch of Yathrib, the faithful lost a good many men in the war against Jahilia... And after the end of the war, hey presto, there was the Archangel Gibreel instructing the surviving males to marry the widowed women..... Salman cried, we were even told it didn't matter if we were already married, we could have up to four marriages if we could afford it, well, you can imagine, the lads really went for that. What finally finished Salman with Mahound: the question of the women; and of the Satanic verses. Listen, I'm no gossip, Salman drunkenly confided, but after his wife's death Mahound was no angel, you understand my meaning.... Those women up there: they turned his beard half-white in a year.... he went for mothers and daughters, think of his first wife and then Ayesha: too old and too young, his two loves.'

(p. 366).

'How many wives? Twelve, and one old lady, long dead. How many whores behind the Curtain? Twelve again;....... When the news got around Jahilia that the whores of the Curtain had each assumed the identity of one of Mahound's wives, the clandestine excitement of the city's males was intense;.... So, in the Prophet's absence, the men of Jahilia flocked to the Curtain, which experienced a three hundred per cent increase in business..... The fifteen-year-old whore 'Ayesha' was the most popular with the paying public, just as her namesake was with Mahound.'

(pp . 380/381).

Rushdie also mocks the idea that Muhammad(sa) would go into trances when he wanted revelations to be sent to suit his needs; for example, in the case of polygamy Rushdie treats the subject lecherously:

'He told Baal about a quarrel between Mahound and Ayesha,... 'That girl couldn't stomach it that her husband wanted so many other women,' he said. 'He talked about necessity, political alliances and so on, but she wasn't fooled. Who can blame her? Finally he went into - what else? - one of his trances,

and out he came with a message from the archangel. Gibreel
had recited verses giving him full divine support. God's own
permission to f... as many women as he liked. So there: what
could poor Ayesha say against the verses of God? You know
what she did say? This: 'Your God certainly jumps to it when
you need him to fix things up for you.'

(p. 386).

Rushdie picks on another incident concerning the Holy Prophet(sa)
and Ayesha in the next paragraph to continue his perverted account
in casting doubt using defamatory language. This incident was the
one in which some scandal-mongers tried to taint the noble character
of Ayesha, and it took a revelation from God to put the matter straight
and exonerate Ayesha completely. Rushdie has, as usual, treated
the subject without any sensitivity and has used it to ridicule and to
deride:

'Lemme tell you instead. Hottest story in town. Whoo-whoo!'
... The two young people had been alone in the desert for many
hours, and it was hinted, more and more loudly, that Safwan
was a dashingly handsome fellow, and the Prophet was much
older than the young woman, after all, and might she not therefore
have been attracted to someone closer to her own age?... 'What
will Mahound do?' Baal wanted to know. 'O, he's done it,'
Salman replied. 'Same as ever. He saw his pet, the archangel,
and then informed one and all that Gibreel had exonerated
Ayesha.' Salman spread his arms in worldly resignation. 'And
this time, mister, the lady didn't complain about the convenience
of the verses.'

(pp. 386/387).

Even in the matter of the death of the Holy Prophet(sa), Rushdie
has exacted historical information from somewhere and added his
lewd style with spurious narrations that bring to the fore the subject
of the 'satanic verses' yet again in the guise of Al-Lat thus giving
food to the thought that even at the time of his death the Holy

Prophet(sa) was influenced by one of the three goddesses that had caused all the controversies earlier in his ministry. Describing the demise of the Holy Prophet(sa), Rushdie writes:

'Within an hour the news arrived that the Prophet, Mahound, had fallen into a fatal sickness, that he lay in Ayesha's bed with his head thumping as if it had been filled up with demons... Then she wept, knowing that he was speaking of his death; whereupon his eyes moved past her, and seemed to fix upon another figure in the room.... 'Who's there ?' he called out. 'Is it Thou, Azraeel?' But Ayesha heard a terrible, sweet voice, that was a woman's, make reply: 'No, Messenger of Al-Lah, it is not Azraeel.' And the lamp blew out; and in the darkness Mahound asked: 'Is this sickness then thy doing, O Al-Lat?' And she said: 'It is my revenge upon you, and I am satisfied. Let them cut a camel's hamstrings and set it on your grave.' Then she went, and the lamp that had been snuffed out burst once more into a great and gentle light, and the Messenger murmured, 'Still, I thank Thee, Al-Lat, for this gift.'

(pp. 393/394).

It is almost as if (God forbid), Muhammad(sa) had succumbed to satanic thoughts right at the end of his life. Could these ever be the thoughts of someone who throughout his life had preached the Unity of God with the firmness of faith never witnessed before? Rushdie must have been living in a fools' paradise to insinuate such ludicrous and farcical claims. He fooled no-one in trying to pass all this off as fiction. This has been a deliberate and premeditated attack on anything and everything to do with Islam and it was meant to hurt all Muslims around the world. Salman Rushdie could never have dreamt of this alone; nor could he have taken the risk of inciting the latent passions of the Muslim fundamentalists on his own; unless, of course, he was promised more money than he could handle, more fame than he could live with and promised comprehensive protection should things get out of hand.

111

It would be interesting to look at the aftermath of the reaction to the publication of *The Satanic Verses*, the pronouncement of the fatwa, the explanations and excuses given by Salman Rushdie himself and the continuation of the anti-Islamic theme of the western media.

But, first, I would like to discuss the subject of blasphemy and the burning of books which has accompanied the 'Rushdie Affair' hand-in-hand, and which just might enlighten the reader as to why the Muslims reacted as they did.

CHAPTER FOURTEEN

BLASPHEMY, APOSTASY AND HERESY

THE 'BURNING' ISSUE SURROUNDING
THE SATANIC VERSES

The burning of a few copies of *The Satanic Verses* in Bradford, Yorkshire by some Muslims created sensational headline news in almost all the newspapers in Britain and was shown extensively on television. The action of a handful of angered Muslims was made out to be the standard reaction of all Muslims at large and the overall handling and tone of the subject led to an even greater rift between the West and Islam.

At the outset I would like to point out that true Islam does not condone the actions of the handful of Muslims who took to book-burning to vent their anger and disgust as a form of protest at the contents of the infamous novel. The vociferous incident did not create any sort of physical violence but the Western media were intent on making a mountain out of a mole-hill. Notwithstanding this, what the media has conveniently forgotten to mention is the long line in history of incidents of book-burning by Christians dating back to the Middle Ages. It had been a practice of the Church in immunising their followers against competing belief systems, like Islam and Judaism, by slandering the competition.

Hans Kung, Professor of Dogmatic and Ecumenical Studies at the University of Tubingen, Germany, writes in *Christianity and the World Religions*:

> 'In the high Middle Ages... Europeans had felt great admiration for the superior state of Arab culture, philosophy, science, and medicine, as well as for the economic and military power of Islam..... The Renaissance, however, saw the rise of a tendency to disparage and reject everything Arabian, including the language.... in the face of the increasing military threat to Christendom from the Turks (in 1529).. the Pope ordered the burning of the Arabic text of the Qur'an immediately after its publication in Venice, which was known at the time as 'the whore of the Turks.' ...... Adrian Reland's *De religione mohammedica* (1705), the first reasonably objective work on Islam after Ross's *Pansebeia*, was promptly placed on the Roman Index of prohibited books;'

(p. 20).

The Jews also suffered greatly at the hands of the Christians whose conspiracy of book burning was part of the church's campaign against Jewish blasphemies. The church took the matter with the utmost seriousness, and the Jews lamented the loss or desecration of their holy books. Professor Leonard Levy writes in great detail in his book *Treason Against God*:

> 'Gregory IX ordered the Talmud to be burned throughout Christendom for its alleged blasphemies against Christ and Mary. ... Louis IX delighted in burning the Talmud. In 1248 another huge batch went up in flames in Paris... In Aragon, where the Talmud was not burned, it was confiscated and censored. Jews were required to turn in all their writings under sentence of death for blasphemy if they failed to comply.... In the 1550s Jewish books as well as rare rabbinic manuscripts were burned by the hundred thousand in Italian cities.... As late as 1629 an Italian cardinal boasted of having collected ten thousand outlawed Jewish books for destruction.'

(pp. 116/117).

Similar narrations are noted by Rev. I.B. Pranaitis in *The Talmud Unmasked*, which is a book about the secret rabbinical teachings concerning Christians:

'In 553, the Emperor Justinian forbade the spread of the Talmudic books throughout the Roman Empire. In the 13th century Popes Gregory IX and Innocent IV condemned the books of the Talmud as containing every kind of vileness and blasphemy against Christian truth, and ordered them to be burned because they spread many horrible heresies.'

(p. 21).

In view of all these historical facts, does it now become a little easier for the West to understand the passionate Muslim reaction to Salman Rushdie's portrait of Muhammad(sa) in *The Satanic Verses*? Does it now seem less incredible that a novel could inspire such hatred and animosity ? Does this now allay the fears of people in the West that Muslim communities do not live in their own cities according to alien values and are ready to defend them to the death?

For those astute enough to be aware of the historical facts, this tragic affair must have served as an uncomfortable reminder of the Western past. Furthermore, the public was left in ignorance, and so when they watched the Muslims of Bradford burning the novel they did not relate this to the bonfires of books that had blazed in Christian Europe over the centuries, but they related this as proof of the incurable intolerance of Islam, a picture that has been painted for centuries.

The members of the general public, especially the British, are a very fair-minded people and when things are presented before them in a rational form, they do judge autonomously and fairly; but if facts are presented with prejudice and couched in a disdainful disguise, as is the wont of the majority of the western media, then it is no surprise that the public sways with the views of those who control this most powerful of mediums.

115

BLASPHEMY AND FREEDOM OF SPEECH

There is an undeniable link between blasphemy and the burning of offensive books. The 'Rushdie Affair' has certainly triggered both, and raised a far more important question as regards freedom of speech. In this section I shall comment, giving examples, on the early cases of blasphemy, their connection to contemporary incidents and the true Islamic teaching on the subject.

Historically the word 'blasphemy' has functioned as an epithet to aggravate or blacken an opinion on sacred matters that is objectionable to one who differs. He may genuinely feel that his religion has been assaulted, yet the 'blasphemy' may exist only in his mind and not necessarily in that of the offender.

THE TEACHING IN THE BIBLE

The Bible is unequivocal in its condemnation of blasphemy. It advocates death for the blasphemer. Leviticus 24:16 fixed the precedent in Judeo-Christian history for punishing blasphemy as a crime:

> 'He who blasphemes the name of the Lord shall be put to death; all the congregation shall stone him; the sojourner as well as the native, when he blasphemes the Name, shall be put to death.'

For centuries, the Jews bore the brunt of the Church's strict and scrupulous adherence to the blasphemy laws; however, no-one was safe from this edict, not even Christians themselves. An ironic example is that of Giordano Bruno, the foremost philosopher of the Italian Renaissance who lived in the 16th century. His case especially makes interesting reading vis-à-vis the plight of Salman Rushdie.

COMPARISON WITH RUSHDIE

The case of Bruno has an eerie similarity with that of Rushdie in facets of literary expression without any boundaries, in his insistence on having the freedom to air his views no matter how controversial and also in the way that he went into hiding.

Giordano Bruno was neither a scientist nor a theologian; he sought to reconcile science and religion, but his philosophy subverted basic theological premises. He said of himself that he had 'given freedom to the human spirit and made its knowledge free. It was suffocating in the close air of narrow prison-house, whence ,..it gazed at the far-off stars.' (*Ash Wednesday Supper*, Giordano Bruno, 1584).

Rushdie, on his part, sought to reconcile fiction with religion, and his 'philosophy' also subverted basic Islamic beliefs. He also strongly advocated freedom of speech and expression. Theology repelled Bruno because he hated dogmas. At the age of 18 he began to doubt the Trinity. He despised religious symbols, especially the images of saints. He could not conceive of God as three persons or accept the doctrine of incarnation. And when the Dominicans began a process against him for heresy, he fled his native Naples. He shed his monastic name and religious habit, but not his intellectual habit of sceptical inquiry. He claimed a right to 'philosophic freedom' and exercised it boldly.

How remarkably similar is the story of Rushdie. He came from a Muslim background but from a very early age he thought the tenets of Islam too cumbersome and, as has been proven from his early works, he wrote on the restrictive nature of the faith and claimed the right to express his views with total freedom.

In his exile, Bruno roamed from city to city in western Europe, studying, teaching and writing. He wrote book after book. Honours began coming his way. Even the King of France personally awarded him a special lectureship in philosophy. Subsequently he lectured at London, Oxford, Prague, Zurich, and Frankfurt.

So has been the case of Rushdie. During his exile, he too has roamed Europe taking his case to all and sundry for sympathy. He has continued to write and give lectures and has been showered with literary awards by his supporters.

117

Bruno's views and massive assault on Aristotelianism brought him into direct conflict with the church. His differing thoughts violated Scripture but, regardless, he continued to go on with his controversial work.

Bruno finally fell into the hands of the Inquisition when he dared to return to Italy in 1592. He was charged with blasphemy, and at first Bruno defended himself vigorously, denying all charges of blasphemy and heretical errors. He claimed philosophic freedom to argue according to the principles of Nature. However, he conceded that his philosophy might be indirectly opposed to truth according to the faith, but he had never meant to impugn that faith. In the end his inquisitors managed to make him fall to his knees and beg for mercy. 'I hate and detest all the errors I have at any time committed as regards the Catholic Faith and decrees of the Holy Church,' he declared, 'and I repent having doubted anything Catholic.'

(Quotations from Boulting, *Bruno*; pp. 276,277).

Nonetheless, the entreaty failed and Bruno stayed in prison.

Salman Rushdie's tale of woe is strikingly similar. His novel brought him into direct conflict with the Muslim Ulemma and he was charged with blasphemy and heresy. And when confronted about his controversial work, he defended his actions vehemently and expressed his right to freedom of speech; he added, nevertheless, that he had never meant to defame Islam or the Holy Prophet(sa). Later, Rushdie also repented and wished to be taken back into the fold of Islam, but when, in spite of this, the edict of the fatwa was not lifted, he reverted to defending his novel once more and fighting even more forcefully for writers' rights.

Bruno was later moved from Venice to Rome, as the chief inquisitor at the Holy Office said that Bruno was no ordinary heretic; he was regarded as a 'heresiarch' - an originator and leader of heresy. He was kept in the dungeon of the Roman Inquisition for seven years. He was charged again with several counts of heresy and at a final interrogation Bruno declared that he would recant nothing. He was duly sentenced to be burnt at the stake which was executed on February 17, 1600. (*Treason Against God*, Leonard Levy; pp. 152-155).

Rushdie also has dared to come back into the public limelight. After seven years in hiding, he had had enough, and in September 1995 he made his first pre-announced public appearance to promote his newest novel, *The Moor's Last Sigh*. He is totally unrepentant in spite of the fact that the threat of the fatwa is still hanging over his head. Perhaps this is a very brave action on the part of Rushdie, or some might say that this is extremely foolish of him; only time will tell!

The last execution for blasphemy in Great Britain occurred in 1697 under Scottish law. In 1698 the English Parliament passed a new act against blasphemy, reducing the penalties. A new era of freedom of religious expression was heralded in with the next century. From then on the victims of the blasphemy laws tended to be freethinkers, rationalists, agnostics and atheists, and they had begun to rely for their defence on the freedom of the press as well as freedom of religion.

BLASPHEMY IN THE 20TH CENTURY

The twentieth century may not be as great an age of faith as the times when men burned witches, blasphemers, and heretics; but in the early part of the century blasphemy was still regarded as an offence and punishable by imprisonment.

In the 1920's and 1930's, there were a great number of cases of blasphemy throughout the Christian world. For example, in England, a blasphemous atheist was jailed for his coarse obscenities about the Gospels and, in particular, for his description of Jesus(as) entering Jerusalem 'like a circus clown on the back of two donkeys.' (Rex v.Gott, 16 Crim.App.Rep.37; 1922).

In the United States, the State of Maine imprisoned a radical for his insulting rejection of religion generally and of the doctrines of virgin birth and incarnation especially. (State v. Mockus, 120 Maine 84, 1921).

Similarly, the State of Massachusetts prosecuted another radical for simply denying the existence of God and the divinity of Jesus(as). The same state jailed the author of a book on freemasonry for referring to Jesus(as) as immoral. Arkansas convicted the president of the American Association for the Advancement of Atheism for possessing literature that ridiculed the Bible's depiction of the creation. (*New York Times*, February 19, 1926).

Canada found blasphemy in a pamphlet virulently attacking the Roman Catholic Church and, in another case, imprisoned and deported the editor of an agnostic journal for his facetious references to the 'frenzied megalomaniac boastings' of a 'touchy Jehovah whom deluded superstitionists claim to be the creator of the whole universe.' (Canadian Bar Rev., V, May 1927).

It will be interesting to note that in the Canadian 'Jehovah' case, the trial judge, when charging the jury, observed that because 'nothing is more sacred to us than our religion,' any disrespectful language or writing that God-fearing people resent is blasphemy.

Even in Great Britain, a country that values freedom of expression so highly, Christianity is still part of the law of the land. However, Judaism and non-Christian beliefs cannot be blasphemed against. In 1978 a court of appeals sustained a conviction for blasphemy. The culprit was James Kirkup, the editor of an obscure homosexual fortnightly magazine, called *Gay News*, in which he published a poem (The Love That Dares to Speak Its Name) that reads as if it were written by the Roman centurion at the foot of the Cross. In the poem, the centurion and Jesus are homosexuals, and the intercourse between them is explicit and undoubtedly shocking to believers.

Surprisingly, James Kirkup has been called a respectable man of letters by 'distinguished' critics and writers. The prosecutor at the trial, however, was no bigot and he urged an updated version of Lord Coleridge's 1883 test : 'You can say Christ was a fraud or deceiver or Christ may have been a homosexual, provided you say it in a ... decent way.' (The same certainly applies to Rushdie). The prosecutor thought the poem's manner 'so vile that it would be hard for even the most perverted imagination to conjure up anything worse.' It is also interesting to note that the trial judge at the Old Bailey refused to permit the introduction of professional testimony on the literary merit of the poem or its author and praised the jury's verdict of guilty and imposed fines of £1,000 on the paper and £500 on its editor; the judge also sentenced the editor to nine months in prison but suspended that part of the sentence pending an appeal. (The 'Gay News' trial was reported daily in The Times from July 4 to July 12 1977).

One could hope that a similar verdict might have been adjudged on Salman Rushdie's *The Satanic Verses*; but instead praise from all over the literary world commended his blasphemous work and conferred endless awards on him and made him out to be an icon in literary circles. Perhaps imprisonment would be too strong a measure in his case as there are no laws to prevent blasphemers against Islam in Britain, but certainly banning publication and distribution of the book would have been a sensible step, in view of the sensitivity of the issue.

Take a very recent example of a publication of a controversial biography of the 1976 Olympic and world ice skating champion John Curry, who died in 1994 of an Aids-related illness after contracting HIV from a homosexual partner. In the book entitled *Black Ice, the life and death of John Curry*, the author, Elva Oglanby, also claims that Curry was involved in homosexual relationships, drugs and mind-control therapy. The family of John Curry strongly challenged the book's account of his upbringing and one of his brothers, Michael Curry, said that the book 'caused great hurt to my family.'

A spokesman for the publisher Victor Gollancz, part of the Cassell group, confirmed:

'We have received a complaint about the book and we have delayed publication.'

(Times, 28 March 1995).

How understanding of the publisher to delay the publication as it would have hurt the feelings of a handful of the immediate members of John Curry's family. But what of the sensibilities and feelings of millions and millions of Muslims all over the world who were going to be insulted in the worst manner possible by the publication of *The Satanic Verses*. Both the publishers and the author of *The Satanic Verses* were well aware of the hurt that the novel would inflict upon the Muslim world and the repercussions that it would instigate.

Perhaps, it is time now to review seriously the blasphemy laws as 'a law that protects only one religion has no place.' So says Geoffrey Robertson QC, in The Times (25 July 1989). He goes on to make another interesting point that 'Rushdie's own eagerly awaited evidence would be inadmissible' because 'in 1979 the House of Lords decided by a 3-2 majority that an alleged blasphemer's intentions are irrelevant. Only the consequence matters.' Furthermore, Robertson adds that 'literary merit is no defence to a blasphemous libel charge.' He also faults the present laws regarding blasphemy as 'it is so uncertain in scope that nobody can establish in advance whether a publication would constitute an offence.' This shows the blasphemy laws to be weak compared to others like 'the web of prohibitions on obscenity and indecency in the media protect sacred subjects from pornographic representation; the Public Order Act punishes the use of threatening, insulting or abusive words or writing that might provoke a breach of the peace; and several laws specifically punish anyone who disturbs religious devotions.'

It appears to be the case that Muslims generally have a strong adherence to their faith. A faith which encompasses belief in all the prophets of God. As such they will always jump to the defence of their beloved prophets - be it Mohammad(sa), Jesus(as), Moses(as) or any other prophet for that matter. This was clearly exemplified upon the release of the film 'The Last Temptation of Christ'. In fact some argued that the Muslims were more vociferous in their objections than any other religious group. This may be so, but it surely proves that the Muslims are consistent in their beliefs and that they fully respect the prophets of other religions. It would be nice if this feeling was reciprocated. Furthermore, the fact that Britain, a 'Christian' society, allowed the film to be broadcast, sheds some light on the general public's attitude towards religion in general. It is no wonder that they fail to understand the outrage of the Muslims over matters concerning faith!

It would be true to say that the decline in morality world-wide, and especially in Britain, and more and more people turning away from religion has contributed to blasphemy being classed as out-dated and out of fashion. But when in countries and faiths where religion still holds centre stage and the subject of blasphemy is taken most seriously, why then do Western commentators cast aspersions on their beliefs and laws no matter how futile and cruel they may seem.

Take for example the case of two Pakistani Christians sentenced to death for blasphemy in Pakistan in February 1995. This created sensational headline news world-wide and gave another opportunity for the Western media to associate Islam with barbarity and inhumanity. Bernard Levin of The Times wrote a most damaging article regarding the incident entitled shockingly: 'Death for graffiti - Is Islam so fragile a religion that it must kill children for imaginary slurs?'

It is little short of utter amazement that an influential newspaper like The Times can let one of their journalists write such injurious and detrimental material that would have done nothing to improve East/West relations. Comments like : 'I know of no other religion that fears to put itself into the challenge, and it is ironic that the religion which seems to be the most fragile is.. by far the most cruel, violent and mad.' And it ends with a contemptuous warning that 'there will be a revulsion against Pakistan so deep, so long-lasting and so conclusive that the mere name of their country will hardly be heard without being accompanied by a spit.' (The Times, 17 February 1995).

123

No thanks to journalists like Bernard Levin, the 'revulsion' against Pakistan, and against Islam in particular, has been an on-going process, and present-day commentators are just adding more fuel to an already smouldering fire.

ISLAMIC TEACHING ON BLASPHEMY

The Rushdie affair has indeed raised some fundamental issues regarding the moral crimes of blasphemy, apostasy and heresy. The prevalent conception in the West about Islam is of a narrow-minded, intolerant and savage religion which advocates conversion at the point of the sword, and the death penalty for blasphemy. But, as I will explain, this is not the truth.

There is absolutely no Qur'anic teaching which imposes any sanction whatsoever on freedom of expression or conscience. The Holy Qur'an gives full rights to all, irrespective of personal ideology, way of life or creed. It states in Chapter 2, Verse 257:

'There shall be no compulsion in religion.'

Though some people have ascribed their own intolerance and narrow-mindedness to Islam, there is not a shred of evidence in the Holy Qur'an that Islam advocates the death penalty for blasphemy or similar profanities. On the contrary, restriction has actually been placed on Muslims themselves not to insult the idols of idolators; Chapter 6, Verse 109:

'And abuse not those whom they call upon besides Allah.'

And this is despite the fact that idolatry is regarded as the most heinous of sins that anyone can commit. Muslims are, therefore, not even allowed to abuse the most outrageous thing in the eyes of God!

This lofty teaching of the Holy Qur'an finds no comparison even in the 'civilised' world of today. Whilst the Holy Qur'an instructs

Muslims to respect others, the British Common Law demands that everyone should honour their religion. Yet it is Islam which is always condemned as being 'backward'!

There can be no greater blasphemy than against God Almighty Himself. Yet the Holy Qur'an prescribes no punishment for such a grievous blasphemy against God. So how could there be a punishment prescribed for blasphemy against prophets who are mere mortals. An incident in the life of the Holy Prophet(sa) clarifies his own understanding of this issue.

A most heinous blasphemy was committed against the Holy Prophet(sa) himself when he was ruler of Medina. A hypocrite by the name of Abdullah bin Ubayy, whose cherished desire of becoming Chief of Medina was shattered by the arrival of Muhammad(sa), during the course of a campaign blatantly boasted that 'if we return to Medina, the one most honoured (i.e. himself) will surely drive out therefrom the meanest (i.e. referring to the Holy Prophet(sa)) ' (Chapter 63, Verse 9).

The faithful Companions of the Prophet(sa) were outraged, none moreso than Abdullah's own son who was a sincere Muslim. With sword drawn, he implored the Prophet(sa) to grant him permission to slay his own father! Many other Muslims also came to the Holy Prophet(sa), but each and every time he refused and emphatically declared that absolutely no action would be taken against Abdullah for his blatant blasphemy.

This incident, however, does not end here. Many years later, when Abdullah eventually died, the Holy Prophet(sa) himself stood up to conduct his burial proceedings. The Holy Prophet(sa) was well known to be full of compassion, and the milk of human kindness, yet this action of his surprised even some of his most faithful companions.

This is the real Islam as taught in the Holy Qur'an and put into exemplary practice by Prophet Muhammad(sa), whose noble example all Muslims are bidden to follow. A religion should not be judged by the actions and notions of a handful of present-day

125

extremist followers, but rather it should be judged from the more authentic and reliable sources on which the religion is based. Would it be right, for instance, to judge Christianity from the modern-day Catholic-Protestant conflict of Northern Ireland, a war that was being waged in the very name of Christianity ? Or from the 'Christian' atrocities of the Middle Ages such as the Spanish Inquisition where tortures like the 'rack', and an ingeniously horrific device known as the 'Iron Maiden' were used to extract the 'truth'. Was this the Christianity practiced and professed by Jesus who was himself the object of severe and untold persecution ?

Commonsense, sound intellect and a large dose of tolerance still go a long way to creating amity among different faiths, nations and communities. But the Western media took the Rushdie Affair and the edict of the fatwa as a 'green light' to creating further enmity against Islam as passages from different newspapers will expose.

CHAPTER FIFTEEN

THE MEDIA GOES TO TOWN
OVER THE FATWA

There was world-wide condemnation of the fatwa imposed on Rushdie, and rightly so. Ayatollah Khomeini got his authority from himself, and not from the Qur'an. But the attitude of the media has been most damaging. The way that the issue has been represented has left the unknowledgeable non-Muslim population with the impression that Islam does not allow freedom of speech, unlike 'civilised' societies in the West, and that its laws are entrenched in the Middle Ages and have no room in the present day-and-age.

An editorial in The Independent (15 February, 1989) regarded the fatwa as out of date and more like 'a response from the Middle Ages'. The article also suggested, as a comparison, that Christianity had become more tolerant with the passage of time of blasphemous material, and that Islam too should follow suit, and the article ends with a grossly dissolute surrender : 'A multi-cultural society (i.e. Britain)... should be considering the abolition, not the extension of the laws of blasphemy.' But surely just because the 'Christians' do not care does not mean that the Muslims should also follow suit.

Clifford Longley, the Religious Affairs Editor of The Times, reiterates the medieval status of the fatwa in his article on 15 February 1989 : 'The outlook of Islam in the 20th century is not so different from than of Christianity in the 13th or 14th.'

127

Most newspapers have highlighted the views of Muslim extremists in Britain and how they have been crying for the 'blood of Rushdie', and have portrayed this as the norm as regards the feelings of all Muslims. But as explained earlier, the fundamental view is that of a very small minority; but then again, outrageous headlines and book-burning photos sell a lot of newspapers. For example, in The Independent of 18 February 1989, a whole page was devoted to the extremist views of young Muslims in Bradford, entitled 'Holy warriors volunteer to kill,' but the rational and modest views of those Muslims who did not endorse the death penalty were added at the end in fine print.

Anthony Burgess of The Independent (16 February 1989) likens the fatwa to 'Islam's gangster tactics' and does not mince his words in condemning some Islamic laws. He is certainly within his right to express his views but the tone arouses feelings of deep hatred for Islam. As he writes:

> 'They (Muslims) have no right to call for the destruction of Mr. Rushdie's book. If they do not like secular society, they must fly to the arms of the Ayatollah or some other self-righteous guardian of strict Islamic morality.'

Muslims are almost regarded as if from another planet, whose teachings and beliefs do not seem to fit in with the rest of the 'civilised' world.

RELIGION CONFUSED WITH CULTURE?

Robert Kilroy-Silk, a former Labour politician, and presently a TV broadcaster, makes equally damaging remarks against Muslims in Britain; in an article in The Times (17 Feb 1989) his views expressed could have led someone to believe that, perhaps, he had transferred his loyalties from the British Labour Party to the British National Party! In the article entitled 'Defending ethnic majorities', he condemns Britain's timid and 'pusillanimous' response to the Ayatollah's death sentence and Britain's 'constant compromise' to 'resident ayatollahs', with the result that 'British traditions, culture and laws have had to be amended to meet the needs of those with values and morals fashioned in less civilised times and places.'

With the subject of the burning of *The Satanic Verses*, Kilroy-Silk is equally condescending on the uncultured status of the ethnic minorities, especially those from the Indian sub-continent. He seems to have a theory that anything that is un-British in its outlook must be uncultured:

'Yet immediately an ethnic minority complains, they (British political and cultural establishment) are willing to have our reading dictated by the tastes of non-English speaking Muslims, many of them not long out of the villages of Bangladesh.'

He also talks arrogantly about the Western culture 'that has evolved in Britain over the past 1,000 years' and boasts that 'the culture that embraces a parliamentary democracy, in which the values of freedom, justice, fairness and toleration are pre-eminent' must be 'better than one which enjoins the burning of books, that passes a death sentence on a man for having unorthodox views.'

His attack on Islam is complete when he concludes his article with defamatory remarks about some of the laws of Sharia, much in the same way that Salman Rushdie has presented in his novels:

'There is nothing in logic or morality that says we must accept it is permissible for a man to have several wives, that animals should be ritually slaughtered, that young girls be circumcised, and women be treated as chattels. Once we go down that road, we will quickly arrive at the market square where criminals are flogged, adulterers are stoned to death and thieves have their hands chopped off.'

Kilroy-Silk has over-generalised and misrepresented facts deliberately to add sensationalism to his article and has certainly confused religion with culture. He talks about British culture over the past 1,000 years that he is so proud of. Without a doubt, there have been commendable eras of British culture, some of which still prevail, but Mr. Kilroy-Silk should also be aware that a lot of what has happened in those 1,000 years does not bear thinking about; for example, in matters relating to blasphemy, book-burning and the like, it is the Christian nations that had been in the forefront, not just in the past 1,000 but in the past 100 years. (This has been discussed in an earlier part of the book).

It is true to say that all nations and cultures have had their ups and downs and have their good and bad points. The media in the West have gone overboard in condemning one of the unacceptable faces of Muslim fanaticism and equated it with the general view of all Muslims. Kilroy-Silk would have done well to choose his arguments more carefully rather than the smug attitude that he had employed, for in the present-day Western culture there are too many warts to mention.

A personality like Robert Kilroy-Silk, who is a high-profile public figure and extremely influential with a popular regular TV debate programme, should show more tolerance himself, which he says is lacking in Muslims, and choose words more carefully when passing judgement on others. Keith Ward, a Professor of History and Philosophy of Religion at King's College, London University, has also fallen into the trap of over-generalising and not presenting the views of orthodox Muslims who are in the majority, but rather highlighting the more sensational and headline-winning opinions of the trouble-makers who are in the minority. In The Independent of 18 February 1989, he talks of 'the decadence' and 'the violent gifts of modern Islam.' Clifford Longley, in The Times (8 July 1989) ascribes an amazing theory that defies belief with the logic that 'the burning of books leads inexorably to the burning of book shops; talk of killing leads to actual killing.' He also scathes Muslim 'separatism' tendencies to living within their own sphere of life and points out that the only way that Muslims are going to be accepted into society is if they compromise some of their beliefs and culture.

And it would be true to say that quite a number of Muslims have become victims of this almost coercive compromise, some willingly and some due to peer or other pressures. Those that dare to make their views public are applauded by the Western media and are then obliged to be used almost as mercenaries to betray their faith in different forms; for instance, in the form of books, theatrical and TV plays, and films. A prime example, apart from the obvious Rushdie, would be Hanif Kureshi, another British Muslim writer, who also faced the wrath of the Muslim community for offending against the tenets of Islam in his works which include writing a film called My Beautiful Launderette. The film, with strong homosexual elements in it, was about the Pakistani community in London and it created a lot of controversy both in England and America. The film contained the phrase 'our country has been sodomised by the religion', which was the main theme and tone throughout.

Hanif Kureshi wrote for another TV series called The Buddha of Suburbia in which Pakistani culture and the laws in Islam are ridiculed once more; the language used is also vulgar and offensive at times. But this is all excused in the name of art and free expression!

It seems that Muslim writers with controversial views on the Muslim way of life alone are given the opportunity to have their work exposed to the general public and are given prime time on television and are then given rave reviews and published in all the tabloids. But programmes and discussions on the true beauty of Islam are rarely shown; and when they are shown, it is at those times when most decent people are asleep.

Television projected the *Satanic Verses* debate through a number of programmes. Many Muslims who had never before been asked found themselves being called upon to articulate their views on TV. But the overall projection was only to prove that the secularists were right. Programmes like Hypotheticals shown on ITV on 30 May 1989 sucked Muslims into a trap to ridicule them. It did not give them a chance to be fully articulate. It merely wanted them to say what the co-ordinator wanted.

But it would be fair to say that a few programmes did give the opportunity for Muslims to explain their true views. Programmes like Islamic Answers shown on Channel 4 (4 May 1989).

131

It would also be fair to say that some areas of the press did present a sympathetic picture of the Muslims who had suffered great hurt due to the publication of the obnoxious novel. It also has to be said that these comments were few and far between and I had to sift laboriously through the ever-increasing pile of vindictive material.

FAIR COMMENT BY THE MEDIA

Conor Cruise O'Brien, the American correspondent of The Times, wrote a well-balanced article (22 February 1989) entitled *Banning, right and wrong* in which he refers to a letter written by Salman Rushdie to Rajiv Gandhi in protest at the Indian Government banning the importation of *The Satanic Verses*. Rushdie had protested in the letter that was published in The New York Times that 'the book isn't actually about Islam.' O'Brien argues that although 'the book isn't entirely about Islam, (but) large parts of it quite clearly are, and even contain quotations from the Koran.' He goes on to say that 'Rushdie makes the point that the prophet in *The Satanic Verses* is not called Mohammed'. O'Brien sees through the facade and calls the ploy 'just a shade disingenuous' and further explains that Muhammad is 'called Mahound. And if you look up Mahound in the OED you will find: 'The false prophet Mohammed... A false god, an idol... A monster, a hideous creature... Used as a name for the devil.' Hardly expressions that would have a sedative effect on those mobs in the bazaars.

O'Brien is also understanding of the reaction of Khomeini and other Muslims who are only acting according to the beliefs of their faith much in the same way as Jews and Christians did in the past. He says that the 'Ayatollah's death sentence on Rushdie... ought not be incomprehensible to a Christian, or to a Jew. In the Old Testament, God tells Moses: 'And he that blasphemeth the name of the Lord, he shall surely be put to death and all the congregation shall certainly stone him... ' (Leviticus 24.14)' O'Brien adds an engaging comparison: 'So when we take Muslims to task for continuing to hold that blasphemy should be punishable by death, it is as if we are saying: 'How dare you go on beating your wife, now

132

that I have left off beating mine?"

A year after the edict of the fatwa, an editorial comment by The Guardian (14 February 1990) gave a discerning and rational viewpoint in order to create some sort of compromise between the disputing factions. For example, it shows Islam in a compassionate light:

'Islam is not a murderous religion. The Koran itself records the insistence of Prophet Muhammad on dealing kindly with a blasphemer who accused him of being 'the meanest, vilest person'.

The viewpoint also supports the anger expressed by all Muslims who 'are understandably aggrieved by the gratuitous way in which Rushdie has insulted beliefs they hold holy. And they have every right to speak up and berate the author.'

The editorial comment is, however, also judicious in advising the Muslims 'to disassociate themselves from the illegal (under both British and Islamic law) fatwa,' and also astute enough to point out that 'only a militant minority of mullahs have in fact supported the death sentence', and that 'the public has been left with the drear and dangerous impression that they represent a majority.' And this sadly is the lasting impression that still exists due largely to the banding together of all the powerful and influential members of the anti-Islam brigade, namely the western media and the societies of authors world-wide who have turned Rushdie into a hero.

CHAPTER SIXTEEN

RUSHDIE TURNED INTO AN ICON

The literary world has stayed united in its condemnation of the fatwa and in its support for Rushdie. But it seems that to make things more unbearable for Muslims and to rub salt in their wounds, they have vied to make Rushdie into some sort of a hero, a literary icon even; so much so that they recently bestowed on him one of the greatest of all literary awards. He beat 23 past Booker Prize winners to take the very first Booker of Bookers Award on 20 September 1993 for his 1981 novel *Midnight's Children*. An editorial in The Times of 21 September 1993 almost gives the game away by trying to justify the award when it says:

'The award of the first Booker of Bookers to Salman Rushdie's *Midnight's Children* is a just recognition of a magnificent work of fiction. It also reclaims a persecuted novelist from the spiteful shadow of the 'Rushdie Affair' and of *The Satanic Verses*.'

It is almost a prize for being made the scapegoat and for defying the fundamentalists and sticking rigidly to his views.

The facts however tell a different story. Rushdie felt that he had been let down by a lot of people who had promised him much more and in the end he had to revert to going 'bowl-in-hand' to all and sundry for putting pressure on Iran to retract the fatwa. The campaign for this even reached America. On his behalf, famous American writers like Norman Mailer and Arthur Miller heavily lobbied the American President, Bill Clinton, to meet with Salman Rushdie.

Clinton finally agreed to meet with Rushdie at the White House in November 1993, which Alexander Chancellor of The Times calls 'a happening of immense symbolic significance which just might be the beginning of the end of Mr Rushdie's nightmare.' This was done despite the risk, as Chancellor puts it, of 'provoking the Muslim world.' (The Times, 4 December 1993).

And this has been the crux of the matter; hurting the sensibilities of millions and millions of Muslims has not even vexed the minds of Rushdie's supporters and accomplices; what has been imputed the greatest of importance is the right to 'freedom of speech' of one individual who has deliberately and maliciously set out to injure the feelings of those very millions of Muslims.

A similar case, to a lesser degree, is that of Taslima Nasreen, a Bangladeshi feminist writer who also triggered Muslim fury after saying that 'the Koran should be revised thoroughly'. She went into hiding on June 4 1993 after 'the Bangladeshi government ordered her arrest for violating religious sentiment, and Islamic militants issued death threats.' (The Times 14 July1993).

As if bound by the unwritten code of outlaws, Rushdie was obliged to rally support for Nasreen. He had become quite influential in drumming up world-wide support for his own case and he used this for two ends. Firstly, by highlighting Nasreen's predicament, there would be safety in numbers; and secondly, his 'noble' effort would make him out to be 'a knight in shining armour'. With these artful qualities Mr. Rushdie would have done well as a politician!

Nevertheless the fact remains that Rushdie is a wanted man and has been described by some as possibly the most famous living writer (or, more appropriately, the most infamous) thanks to the Iranian fatwa imposed after *The Satanic Verses* was published. Was this all fully intended, or was it just part of the plan that went terribly wrong?

No matter what has been written in the defence of the controversial and blasphemous novel, there is no doubt, as the following evidence shows, that Salman Rushdie knew exactly what he was doing and what he was letting himself in for, and that he had been forewarned by eminent members of the literary world of the dire consequences.

RUSHDIE FOREWARNED

There are many similar reports which unequivocally point the finger at Rushdie for daring to ignore sound advice. According to one report by Tom Kelsey and David Lister the 'publishers of *The Satanic Verses* sought informal advice from religious experts prior to the novel's publication and were warned that it would unleash terror beyond the control of any one person or even one country.' The consensus among the nine referees who included Christians and Jews and who received a draft copy from the publishers three months before publication was 'that the book could not be considered a work of fiction because it used historical figures and would therefore cause a lot of offence... The publishers went ahead regardless'. (The Independent 6 March 1989).

The case of the publishers seems very clear. The more controversy a book could develop, the more sales it would get. This turned out to be a publisher's dream that a book could generate such controversy and publicity. But this dream was soon to turn into a living nightmare. At least for the author, that is. He may have been manipulated by powers greater than he, and he may have been made the scapegoat, but he was not quite as innocent as he has tried to make out.

A MOST POIGNANT OBSERVATION

The motive of Rushdie is certainly under suspicion, and an eminent English author, Roald Dahl, a member of the Society of Authors, and who is perhaps the first non-Muslim to expose bravely Rushdie for what he truly represents, raised a very important question in a letter published in The Times, 28 February 1989. In it he wrote that 'with all that has been written and spoken about the Rushdie affair, I have not yet heard any non-Muslim voices raised in criticism of the writer himself. On the contrary, he appears to be regarded as some sort of hero... To my mind, he is a dangerous opportunist. Clearly he has profound knowledge of the Muslim religion, its people, and he must have been totally aware of the deep and violent feelings his book would stir up among devout Muslims. In other words, he knew exactly what he was doing and he cannot plead otherwise.'

Roald Dahl ends his letter by making a very noteworthy observation which has been missed by most of the western media and Rushdie's supporters : 'In a civilised world we all have a moral obligation to apply a modicum of censorship to our own work in order to reinforce this principle of free speech.'

The Times (20 February 1989) published another article entitled 'Penguin under fire for ignoring expert advice', by Andrew Morgan and Peter Davenport. The article discusses Penguin's consultation with Mr. Khushwant Singh, the Penguin editorial consultant in India in the summer of 1988. He had said that he was positive that the manuscript would cause a lot of trouble. 'There are several derogatory references to the Prophet and the Koran, and Muhammad is made out to be a small-time impostor.' This was following an earlier rejection of the manuscript by him on the grounds that it was 'lethal'. Mr. Singh met with the Penguin Group marketing director in London, who is also chairman of Penguin India. 'He was a little surprised and peeved because they had paid a lot of advance royalties'.

The 'advance royalties', to the tune of a million dollars, certainly makes one sit up and take notice. There must have been something out of the ordinary as regards this novel when you consider that the most lucrative literary award in Britain is only £34,000 for the David Cohen British Literature Prize.

Something was certainly amiss. Such a large amount of money in advance royalties reeks of conspiracy and shady dealings only associated with the Mafia and the like. This payment also suggests that the author was being paid for endangering his life as he was to be involved in the greatest gamble of his life.

And when you consider that the publishing company making the payment is of Jewish predilection and the literary attack is on Islam alone, and nothing against Judaism and Christianity, it does not take a genius to work out the treachery behind it all. Rushdie was the ideal go-between who could easily be bought, at a price of course. He knew how to hurt Muslims the most, as John Ezard of The Guardian observed:

'Salman Rushdie, who was brought up in Islam, knows exactly where to put the needle in.'
(15 February 1989).

AUTHOR OF HIS OWN DESTINY

Much of what has been said and quoted has been to prove that Rushdie was a willing tool that the Christian nations of the West had employed to continue its assault on Islam. Rushdie will of course deny this but his behaviour and excuses reported in the media are all proof that he was the author of his own destiny.

Professor Michael Dummett of New College, Oxford, in an open letter published in The Independent (11 February 1989) addressed to Salman Rushdie, clearly exposes how Rushdie had changed loyalties to go with the highest bidder. Addressing Rushdie, Professor Dummett writes:

'Before *The Satanic Verses* was published , you were a hero among members of the ethnic minorities, far beyond the circle of those who had read your books, for your forceful television broadcast denouncing British racism.... It was your status as a hero that made your book appear so great a betrayal. Much as you might want to, you can never again play that role: you can never again credibly assume the stance of denouncer of white prejudice. For now you are one of us. You have become an honorary white: merely an honorary white intellectual, its is true, but an honorary white all the same.'

Professor Dummett also makes the accusation against Rushdie that:

'if you really did not grasp the offence you would give to believing Muslims, you were not qualified to write upon the subject you chose. In any case, no one escapes responsibility for the consequences of a bad action by having failed to foresee them; moreover, you know now, yet you still insist on your right to wider publication.'

CHAPTER SEVENTEEN

RUSHDIE'S DEFENCE OF
THE SATANIC VERSES

After the fatwa was declared, Rushdie entered into different phases of fickle explanations for writing the infamous novel. One moment he was defending the book; another moment he was apologising for the hurt he had caused; and yet another moment he was totally unrepentant. The period from the pronouncement of the fatwa to the present will show the mercurial changes in the character of Rushdie and how the true character surfaces.

Immediately after the death sentence was imposed, Rushdie in fear of his life, defended his book saying that it 'was not an attack on Islam or any other religion. It was an attempt to challenge preconceptions and to examine the conflict between secular and religious views of the world.' (The Times, 15 February 89).

So much for it being a work of fiction! Rushdie appeared on Channel 4 in a programme broadcast by Bandung File on 14 February 1989 in which he was unyielding in defending his views. He half-expected the reaction of the Muslims:

'I expected that the mullahs wouldn't like it. But I didn't write it for the mullahs. I've seen what the mullahs have done in Pakistan over the past 11 years.... I insist on my right to express it as I think fit.'

He seems to know a lot about the mullahs; he should also know that the mullahs have an alarming influence on the masses, and so consequently, the reaction of the masses would be synonymous to theirs. So, in spite of knowing the hurt that it would cause, he carried on regardless in the name of 'freedom of speech'.

He also makes the futile assumption that 'if you don't want to read a book, you don't have to read it. It's very hard to be offended by *The Satanic Verses*; it requires a long period of intense reading. It's a quarter of a million words.' This smug assumption is as futile as it is unjustified. It would not be long before he would have to come up with better explanations to pacify the volatile situation that he would find himself in.

When asked about the controversy about acting and playing on the historic text of the Qur'an, he clearly admits that it was almost entirely based on historical fact. For example, he says:

> 'Almost everything in those sections - the dream sequences - starts from an historical or quasi-historical basis, though one can't really speak with absolute certainty about history when you talk about that period of Mohammed's life.... The interesting thing about Mohammed is that there is objective information about him other than the sacred text.'

Rushdie then goes on to say that the reason for the book was to explore themes that would answer two questions. 'When an idea (like Islam) comes into the world, it's faced with two big tests: when you're weak, do you compromise; when you're strong, are you tolerant?' He clearly talks about Muhammad(sa) in answering these questions:

> 'as far as we can tell about Mohammed's life... there seems to have been a brief flirtation with a possible compromise- about monotheism - which was very rapidly rejected.'

How audacious and impertinent of Rushdie to keep insisting that this work can be deemed fictional when he clearly admits that it was Muhammad(sa) that he was writing about; and the fact that 'Mahound' is used to refer to Muhammad(sa) is a clear indication of the deliberate attempt to provoke Muslims. (An edited extract was published in The Guardian, 15 February 1989).

Rushdie contends that 'Mahound' is not the Prophet Muhammad(sa) but a figment of his character Gibreel's sleeping mind. Even were this so, Rushdie's defence breaks down on theological grounds. Professor Yaqub Zaki points out that 'the Prophet is the one creature in the whole of creation God does not allow the Devil to impersonate; therefore, when you have a dream of the Prophet you know it must be true.' (The Times, 28 February 1989).

Zaki makes another interesting point that exposes Rushdie's guile in choosing the title name of the book : "Rushdie's use of the name of the devil responsible for the fraud is intended to indicate that the whole Koran is fraudulent and Muhammad a mean impostor: not a question of two verses spotted as such but all the 6,236 verses making up the entire book. In other words the title is a 'double entendre'." (Yaqub Zaki, formerly James Dickie, is a British Muslim author and a visiting professor at Harvard University).

RUSHDIE ISSUES STATEMENT

It is also evident from Rushdie's begrudging statement that he issued that his ploy had worked in achieving what he had set out to do. Note also the hollow and hypocritical tone of the statement, the full text of which is:

'As author of *The Satanic Verses* I recognise that Muslims in many parts of the world are genuinely distressed by the publication of my novel. I profoundly regret the distress that publication has occasioned to sincere followers of Islam. Living as we do in a world of many faiths this experience has served to remind us that we must all be conscious of the sensibilities of others.'

(The Times, 20 February 1989).

This statement was made only a few days after the author is on record as having said:

'Frankly I wish I'd written a more critical book... it seems that Islamic fundamentalism could do with a little criticism right now.'

(The Washington Times, 15 February 1989).

RUSHDIE'S SUPERFICIAL REVERSAL

After nearly two years in hiding, Salman Rushdie changed his tune somewhat. Perhaps it was due to international pressure, or for reasons dictated by conscience and guilt, or maybe it was due to plain cowardice. Rushdie sanctioned a statement which said that he accepted that there was no God but Allah and that Muhammad(sa) was His last prophet. Ruth Gledhill, the Religious Affairs reporter of The Times (27 December 1990) wrote about Rushdie's 'disavowal of statements in his book *The Satanic Verses*. Rushdie's disavowal, which came after a Christmas Eve meeting with Muhammad Ali Maghoub, an Egyptian minister for religious endowments, and other senior Muslim figures, also included the following:

'he did not agree with any statement in his novel uttered by any of the characters who insult the Islamic faith. He undertook not to publish the paperback edition of *The Satanic Verses* or to permit further translations during the conflict.'

This clearly discloses evidence that there was offensive material against Islam in the novel and that he was fully aware of it. He concluded his disavowal by promising:

'I will continue to work for a better understanding of Islam in the world, as I have always attempted in the past.'

Rushdie wrote an article in The Times of 28 December 1990 explaining his earlier disavowal under the heading 'Why I have embraced Islam'. Perhaps this was imposed on himself due to the fear of the ever-hanging edict of the fatwa, or it may have been true repentance. It may also have been the fact that he was disappointed with the non-action of the British Government in endorsing sanctions against Iran to put pressure on the latter to revoke the fatwa and he felt that there was nothing left now but to come out in the open and to try and compromise with the Muslim world himself. He started by giving feeble excuses for his un-Islamic upbringing:

'Although I come from a Muslim family background, I was never brought up as a believer, and was raised in an atmosphere of what is broadly known as secular humanism.'

He continues:

'I am certainly not a good Muslim. But I am able now to say that I am a Muslim; in fact it is a source of happiness to say that I am now inside, and a part of, the community whose values have always been closest to my heart.'

He then feebly tries to defend his novel:

'For over two years I have been trying to explain that *The Satanic Verses* was never intended as an insult and that the assaults on religion are representative of (the) process of ruination of the central character of the book, and not representative of the point of view of the author.'

The irony is that he admits to there being offensive material in the book and disowns it as not being his viewpoint. Perhaps it is representative of the 'point of view' of his manipulators who paid him in advance to write this novel.

The more one reads his statement, the more one becomes aware of Rushdie desperately clutching at straws. On the one hand he is making flimsy excuses, defending his literary work and its 'fictional' content and to be accepted back into the Muslim brotherhood, while on the other hand he wants the book to be accepted for what it is. The article is full of contradictions, especially two statements which appear almost side by side:

144

Statement 1:

'As a contribution to that new atmosphere of goodwill, I have agreed not to permit new translations of The Satanic Verses, nor to publish an English-language paperback edition, while any risk of further offence remains.'

Statement 2:

'I believe the book must continue to be available, so that it can gradually be seen for what it is. I will discuss with Penguin Books the possibility of adding to the existing hardback editions a statement declaring that it is not intended as an attack on Islam.'

The very fact that Rushdie had agreed to add this statement proves that, intended or not, there is material that attacks Islam. Another part of the article gives rise to some probing questions. The part of the statement relates to the six Muslim scholars that Rushdie met on Christmas Eve to make his disavowal:

'They agreed that over the past 15 years I have in fact shown myself to be an ally of Muslims, whether in Kashmir, or the rest of India, or Palestine or in Britain, where I have frequently written and broadcast against all forms of discrimination.'

If he sees himself as someone who had championed the cause of Islam, how could he have then betrayed the trust of those very Muslims that he was speaking out for by publishing a novel that damages the name of Islam?

Firstly, his statement that hints at his sympathetic feeling towards Islam is ill-founded. In all his previous books that span a period of 20 years, I have quoted references which quite categorically show his utter contempt for Islam.

Secondly, even if you give him the benefit of the doubt and accede that he is really a Muslim and that he has at times spoken in support of Islam's beliefs, then how can it be conceivable that he could write a book so damaging to the name of Islam that would create the biggest scandal and offence in literary history?

145

It certainly makes one wonder and sit up and take notice. All the evidence surely points to a conspiracy where bigger 'guns' than Kashmir, India and Pakistan put together backed Rushdie and employed his literary style of fictional wordplay to achieve their evil goals while at the same time promising him wealth and fame he could not have dreamed of.

And Rushdie all but names his co-conspirators in another part of his statement where he seems to have at heart the interests of a minority rather than the interests of the majority of Muslims world-wide when he defends his decision not to withdraw the book:

'*The Satanic Verses* is a novel that many of its readers have found to be of value. I cannot betray them.'

How noble of him to care for the sensibilities of a few people at the expense of millions! Rushdie's true colours are loudly exposed. He had made an unwritten pact with the enemies of Islam and he not only 'cannot' but he 'dare' not betray them. Rushdie, the mercenary who grasped the opportunity offered to him with both hands, did not care in the least that he would be betraying the trust of all Muslims in the world for whom he had hypocritically admitted amity. One certainly begins to wonder, as in the time-old adage, that with friends like Rushdie, who needs enemies?

Rushdie ends his statement with his tongue firmly in his cheek when he appeals to all Muslims to join in the process of healing that he says has begun: 'What I know of Islam is that tolerance, compassion and love are at its very heart.'

In all his books to date the message of Islam according to him has been the antithesis of the above statement and he must take Muslims for fools if he thought that they would fall for this condescending plea.

He also believes that 'the language of enmity will be replaced by the language of love'. How mockingly tedious is his wish; it is the foul and vindictive language used in his book that has to be replaced and until that is done few Muslims will ever be able to forgive him or hold any meaningful dialogue with him. The ball

146

was now very much in Mr. Rushdie's court!

As time went by Rushdie became more and more anxious, as there seemed to be no relenting on the edict of the fatwa. His time in exile had, understandably, become unbearable. He used whatever opportunity he was allowed to vent his views and he used them to the full with the Western media always at his side. He felt that the British Government had betrayed him and that it had sidelined his case; he expressed this quite openly to attract sympathy because he knew that his only hope of being protected was behind the shield of a powerful government like Britain.

He was invited to give a speech at the Stationer's Hall in London on 14 February 1992, the edited version of which appeared in The Times the next day, headlined 'I must not be forgotten'. This was a direct call to Britain not to sell him out:

'I have no wish to be in adversarial relationship with the British government, because it has protected me and remains my best hope of a solution, but I wish that the government would make it a little easier for me to believe that they're strongly and resolutely on my side.'

He even has the audacity to make specific demands and urges the government that 'any deal with Iran which excludes a full, public and effective settlement of the Rushdie case will be unacceptable.'

Perhaps the reason why he is so daring in exacting demands on the government is that he had been promised beforehand that the situation would never reach the extreme stage that it now had. Obviously he cannot name any names.

He was like an agitated, wounded animal in a cage, not knowing which way to turn. His weak and feeble attempt to be accepted back into the Muslim community had failed miserably; everyone saw through his insidious and guileful embrace of Islam. This is borne out in greater detail in a rare interview that Rushdie gave to Anne McElvoy of the Times published on 26 August 1995, which will be interesting to read in the interviewer's own words:

147

'Once, he tried to make amends with his enemies. At Christmas 1990, he converted to Islam, a move he now describes as 'the biggest mistake of my life'. Brought up in a relaxed Muslim home, he abandoned the faith as a teenager and retains a cultural, although not a spiritual, affinity with it. 'At the time, I was trying to protect *The Satanic Verses* as the work of someone who really knew Islam. But is was wrong, because I don't believe in God, so I should not have suggested that I did.'

His only hope lay with the very conspirators who had in part been responsible for putting him where he found himself now. And at the same time he was reverting to his original defence of his book:

'*Satanic Verses* is a serious novel, a moral novel ... It is neither filthy nor degrading nor abusive ... It is a work of art.'

How can a work of fiction be considered 'serious' and 'moral'?

Another statement he makes in his speech is like a self-inflicted nail in his own coffin. In talking about freedom of speech and expression he compares himself to other Muslim writers in Islamic countries:

'A distinquished Saudi novelist is stripped of his citizenship, and what's the charge? He has been anti-Islamic. An Egyptian novelist, his publisher and printer are jailed for eight years, and what's the charge? Blasphemy again. They too, have been anti-Islamic.'

By comparing himself to these Muslim writers, he has admitted to being in the same boat as them and has inadvertently charged himself with being anti-Islamic, something that he has tried to deny all along.

Clearly his time in hiding has been devoted largely to drumming up support world-wide in trying to neutralise the situation that was on the brink of the perilous as well as the ludicrous. There was no shortage of support from the Western literary world for whom he had become a symbol of the freedom of speech and expression. During this time in hiding he also found time to write some more books, and again there was assistance readily available. The first of his books since his exile was *Haroun and The Sea of Stories*, published in 1990.

HAROUN AND THE SEA OF STORIES

This is supposed to be a children's book as it is designated to that section of the library. The publishers were again Penguin, but I am sure that they must have stipulated that they were not quite ready for another episode of the occurrences that ensued the publication of Rushdie's previous novel, and that he should play safe and write a not-too provocative one, at least for the time being.

This novel was pretty ineffectual and the main reason for it, apart from the financial aspect, was a reminder and a clarion call for all the writers of the 'free' world to continue their pursuit of procuring justice for Rushdie. Rushdie could still not resist the temptation of having yet another jibe at falsely accusing the Muslim law of restricting freedom of thought and independence. He uses his conventional style of trying to disguise his message in fictional terms, but the intimation is easily discernible. For example, in trying to say that Muslims are restricted in expressing their true views and feelings and that they live in a state of submissiveness, he uses the Hindi term Chup City (a silent city) for the Islamic world and the term Bezaban (without a tongue) for its inhabitants, that is the Muslims.

The world that Rushdie obviously belongs to is none other than Gup City where gossip and nonsense abound. (Rushdie is kind enough to give meanings of the Hindi words at the end of the book for the children). Furthermore, I am sure he is referring to himself in the book when he writes that Rashid Khalifa, the central character, is 'awarded the Land of Gup's highest decoration, the Order of the Open Mouth, in recognition of his exceptional services'. (p. 192).

In Chapter 12 of the book entitled 'Was It the Walrus?', Rushdie relates a mock trial of the right to express freedom of speech and wishfully records a victory for his cause. His hopes and aspirations for a happy ending for himself and his colleagues are also vividly expressed:

149

'You said it could be a big wish, and so it is. I come from a sad city, a city so sad that it has forgotten its name. I want you to provide a happy ending, not just for my adventure, but for the whole sad city as well.'

(p. 202).

Rushdie keeps stressing that he is fighting for the right of freedom of speech of all writers but his struggle has been purely for selfish reasons. He certainly falls short of standards applied to heroic behaviour. So says his former wife, Marianne Wiggins, who 'proved as much when she attacked him for failing to lend the weight of his case to the cause of less well known threatened writers and anti-racism, saying, 'All of us wish that the man had been as great as the event. That's the secret everyone is trying to keep hidden. He is not.' (Anne McElvoy, The Times, 26 August 1995).

She is certainly right in saying that the secret is well-hidden because the praise and the glory seem to be coming from all directions.

In the same way that his previous works have been overly praised, so as a sense of obligation the unified band of literary critics overstress the quality of this novel. For example, in the review at the beginning of this novel there are numerous quotations glorifying the talent of Rushdie : 'a work of literary genius', (Stephen King); 'Rushdie's most eloquent and compelling gesture as writer, father and citizen', (Edward Said, Independent on Sunday); 'a great tribute to the resilience of Mr Rushdie's beleaguered spirit', (Anthony Burgess, Observer); 'a children's classic; keep your first edition carefully to bequeath to your grandchildren', (Victoria Glendinning, The Times).

But I suppose the critic from India Today exposes the author's real motive for writing this book when it is regarded as a 'lyrical defence of his artist's license, so rudely and terminally impounded by the Islamic gendarmes.'

This point is re-iterated by A.N. Wilson of The Sunday Telegraph claiming that the book 'shines like a bright light in a world increasingly fearful of freedom or ideas.' Rushdie continued the 'lyrical defence of his artist's license' in his next novel called *East, West* which was published in 1994.

EAST, WEST

This was also a children's novel, and just as the title suggests it is a mixture of stories and fables from the East and the West. He exposes all the crude and savage customs of the East and gives the impression of them being the norm. In one fable called 'The Prophet's Hair', the Islamic mode of worship is ridiculed again as in his previous books; but this time he does not defame the Holy Prophet(sa). He talks of prayers and the reading of the Holy Qur'an as a sort of penance for the children. Perhaps he is trying to dissuade western children from appreciating the true qualities of Islam, by presenting a false picture of the normal life of a young Muslim.

On the other extreme, another story entitled 'Christopher Columbus and the Queen Isabella of Spain Consummate Their Relationship', a sexual tale, is presented in an enchanting manner which really shows the irresponsibility of the author. If this was not enough, the language also is depraved and offensive, considering this is supposed to be a children's novel. For example, in the story entitled 'The Courtier' he has reverted to use the 'F' word no less than ten times within a space of a few lines. (pp. 204/205). I suppose this was done for the sake of 'art'!

Salman Rushdie seems always to have believed and still continues to believe that with a writer's license he is free to do as he wishes, and the fact that he is being bestowed honours and being applauded all the way to the bank seems to make his ego get even bigger by every book that he writes.

CHAPTER EIGHTEEN

RUSHDIE BEGINS TO COME
OUT IN THE OPEN

With the 'Rushdie Affair' no longer being considered as a high-profile topic for the media, Salman Rushdie slowly began to make in-roads to appear on television to appeal to a larger audience and to continue the fight for writers' freedom of speech and expression. He started to travel all around the western world to achieve some sort of success.

For instance, he accompanied Taslima Nasreen, the Bangladeshi feminist writer in almost the same predicament as himself, to attend a symposium on free expression in Norway in September 1994. A month later he was invited to Germany to meet European Union foreign ministers to take his case further. (This was also seen as a gesture against Muslims.)

On Monday 1 October 1994 he appeared on a BBC2 television programme called Face to Face in which Jeremy Isaacs questioned him on a subject about how far writers are justified in giving offence, with special reference to *The Satanic Verses*. If anything, and despite the Iranian death threat, Rushdie was less apologetic than ever. Indeed he mounted a sturdy defence of the writer's freedom to explore contentious areas and said that the easiest way not to be offended by a book is to shut it. What an irrational and fatuous idea! Does this mean that people should be allowed to perform lewd and lavatorial acts in public and if you are offended by it then you should close your eyes?

Rushdie's public appearances began to be regular, but it was not until 7 September 1995 that he dared to make his first pre-announced appearance since his exile in 1989. This was at The Times/Dillons debate, - 'Writers Against the State', held in Westminster Central Hall, London, to mark the publication of his new novel *The Moor's Last Sigh*. At the debate he openly declared that one of the aims of the writer is to create controversy deliberately and say the unsayable:

'We will not allow priests to tell us when we have to shut up. Part of our function is to stir things up a bit.... stirring things up is our proper function in any society.'

(The Times, 8 September 1995).

And that is exactly what he has done in *The Moor's Last Sigh*. Just when the world was about to give a big sigh of relief, Rushdie has stirred things up yet again. This time he has upset the Hindus, and especially Bal Thackeray, head of Shiv Sena, one of India's most feared extremist religious groups.

The novel relates a cartoonist's unnerving rise to become an evil political leader. His resemblance to Thackeray, who is motivated by a powerful contempt for Muslims, has been missed by nobody. This novel should also not be mistaken as a defence of Islam; far from it. It is to do with the wide-ranging theme of religious intolerance, and basically Rushdie's stance on religion does not change - he is still very much averse to it.

It seems that the 'Rushdie of old' is re-emerging, more intent than before; making up for lost time, as it were! With the passage of time the fear to express himself fully once again seems to have left him, rekindling the freedom he flaunted in *Midnight's Children* in which he discovered the power that he had acquired through literary expression and which made him remark:

'It was astonishing how soon fear left me.'

(p. 162).

153

'Think before you leap' is an aphorism that never entered the mind of Rushdie, whose sole aim in writing had been to bask in glory. In his own words:

'I prefer glorious failure to modest success.' He said this to Kate Kellaway of The Observer in The Waterstone's Magazine of Autumn 1995. When asked if there was anything that he had to think twice about saying, he makes an equally asinine statement:

'If I ever felt that, I would stop writing. I have too much respect for the art of the novel to become a censor of myself. If I felt that I was holding back, I'd stop because good literature happens at the edge and if you're scared of going near it, you can't write it.'

He sees safety as desirable in life, undesirable in fiction. 'I've never been the kind of writer who would deliberately put myself in a place of great unsafety.'

What an incredible and fallacious statement. It seems that the time in exile has stripped Rushdie of his sanity. All the facts point to the exact opposite that Rushdie, knowingly and deliberately, has put himself in the predicament that he finds himself in. It is only the extremity of the situation that he had overlooked.

Another statement that he makes: 'If you do not take risks, you can't do anything interesting', seems to be the criterion applied to all his work, including his latest *The Moor's Last Sigh*. This ostensibly has given him the right to 'stir things up' at the expense of any eventualities.

Rushdie will no doubt be extremely pleased with the hostile reaction in India to his latest novel and, in particular, how it has offended Bal Thackeray who is parodied as a villainous thug, and whose supporters have claimed that they will destroy any copies of the book and have threatened anyone selling it. This has provoked controversy reminiscent of *The Satanic Verses*. Bal Thackeray, ironically, was among prominent Indians who defended Rushdie over *The Satanic Verses*. Thackeray, at that time, condemned India's banning of *The Satanic Verses* and said 'freedom of speech was

154

more important than the feelings of any religious group'. (Sunday Times, 3 September 1995).

How quickly the principles of 'free speech' are forgotten when one oneself becomes the victim of a writer's venomous pen. It must become doubly painful when one considers that one had been supportive of the same writer for another piece of work that had endangered the life of the writer. But this comes as no surprise when you consider the doubtful character of the writer, who had long before rid himself of all scruples, and who was only intent on hankering after his own interests.

NOBEL PRIZE FOR RUSHDIE?

The reward for Rushdie for 'stirring things up' yet again could well have been another Booker Prize, for which he was said to be favourite by the literary critics. Andy Miller of Waterstone's called it 'a sure-fire bet for the Booker Prize'; but Guy Walters of The Times put Rushdie on a much higher pedestal for the fact that he was in line for a third Booker Prize. 'To win one Booker Prize may be regarded as cleverness, to win two looks like genius, and to win three will be an act of deification.' (The Times, 5 October 1995).

Rushdie has already, in 1994, been named as the first President of the International Parliament of Writers, to add to his already growing number of international honours and decorations. With this third Booker Prize also almost under his belt, the next obvious step in Rushdie's rapid rise to the dizzy heights of fame and glory would have been the Nobel Prize for Literary Fiction!

The judges should, however, be warned. Rushdie does not take defeat with honour. Philip Howard, the literary editor of The Times, mentions the debacle that followed the failure of one of his earlier novels, *Shame*, to win the Booker Prize after it was made the favourite to do so:

'It (*Shame*) was the favourite to win the Booker. When it did not, Rushdie took it badly. He leapt to his feet and harangued

155

the judges and passers-by.'

(The Times, 15 February 1989).

Perhaps it was this intense passion and desire for fame and glory that Rushdie flaunted which made him the target for the Judaeo-Christian conspirators against Islam, who then took him under their wing and slowly but surely nurtured him to become part of their spiteful and implacable crusade to further defame and distort the name of Islam.

Much to Rushdie's disappointment, he just failed to win the Booker prize with *The Moor's Last Sigh*. In spite of this he received great support from his close band of followers, like Auberon Waugh, editor of The Literary Review, who said that a man who had been chased 'from pillar to port by religious maniacs' deserved victory (The Times, November 1995). The fact that Waugh admitted that he had not even read Rushdie's novel just adds absurdity to the blinkered and fanatical support he still has, just to reward him in the name of freedom of speech.

And Rushdie should also be prepared, if he wins the Nobel Prize, to share it with his co-conspirators, as they have been instrumental in making him the celebrity that he is now!

But facts have borne out that this could never be expected from a being whose only purpose in life has been pure self-aggrandisement. And what is also very evident is the fact that Rushdie cannot digest any accusations or aspersions cast on him, thus decrying his principle of freedom of speech for every writer. I will illustrate the contradiction of this very principle that Rushdie has been so assiduously waging a crusade for.

WHO KILLED THE WRITER?

It is quite obvious that Rushdie and his supporters in the literary field have been stretching the theme of freedom of the writer to the limit and beyond. Note, for example, the statement issued by Rushdie

156

himself on the subject:

> 'Nowhere in the entire catalogue of human rights will you find the Right Not To Be Offended. If such a right existed, all of us would be silenced. Offence is not, and must never be, a reason for censorship in a free society.'
>
> (The Times, 15 February 1992).

Yet, Rushdie's reaction to a fictitious play that presupposes his death was typically selfish and devoid of the very principles that he has been crusading for since the fatwa.

Brian Clark, the playwright, wrote a play *Who Killed The Writer?* following the fatwa, in order that 'writers should immediately do what they could to express support, and, more importantly, draw the lessons from the event.' He wanted to show 'through a confrontation between the assassin and a political journalist' that even though Rushdie's "condemnation by the Ayatollah was wicked and unacceptable in any kind of world order we can tolerate, it did not arrive out of the blue, but that the Western powers have helped to create the monster which now threatens to devour us."

This was part of the covering letter that Brian Clark sent to Salman Rushdie with a copy of the play before the title became known, in the hope that it would reassure him that:

> 'while I have used your appalling predicament, I have not exploited it.... I have only one hope for the play and that is by widening the debate about Muslim (or any other) fundamentalism, I may contribute to a general lessening of tensions in the world.'

This seemed like a noble enough gesture by a fellow writer, but the response by Rushdie has once again exposed his true self-motivated perverse character. Brian Clark continues:

> 'Mr Rushdie responded by leaving a message on my answer-phone saying he was appalled that I would think the play which postulated his death could in any way be acceptable to him, that he would resist its being performed.'

Furthermore, Brian Clark was 'shocked to be in receipt of a letter from Mr Rushdie's agent saying that if we intended production we should send him a formal note so that he could establish Salman's legal rights.'

Brian Clark decided in the end not to go ahead with the production; in spite of this he writes that he received no note from Rushdie to acknowledge his concession and feels now that his 'act of self-censorship was misguided.'

Clark's assertion is probably shared by many fair-minded people when he surmises: 'The irony of Mr Rushdie wishing to suppress a play because it offended him was so obvious that it became clear to me that he could not be thinking well.' (The Independent on Sunday, 11 February 1990).

The truth of the matter is that Mr. Rushdie has not been 'thinking well' since the beginning of his literary career, and his vision has been clouded by the lure of fame and money, reaching its zenith with the publication of *The Satanic Verses*.

CONCLUSION

Rushdie has become the self-appointed voice of the freedom of all writers and has issued himself the license to do as he wishes.

In view of this and all the happenings recorded in the last few years it can be deemed, quite undeniably, that rather than Salman Rushdie being afforded protection from the people he offends, it is the general public that needs to be protected from his poisoned pen and from other writers of similar proclivity. It has become an amusing avocation for them to hurt, and gibe at the things and beliefs that others hold so dear and precious.

Rushdie had been gradually built up to a high-profile personality - something that he could very easily relate to. Even his close friends have remarked that 'he is not a man given to underestimating his own importance'. He even has the arrogance 'to suggest that meeting him' would be 'one of the great moments of (anyone's) life.' (The Times Magazine, 26 August 1995).

Throughout the whole episode of the nefarious affair, Rushdie has displayed a mottled and confused character verging on the shameful and rancorous; his ardent supporters, however, have elevated him to displaying iridescent and romanesque qualities that would win the adoration and sympathy of the masses which would, in turn, in a perverted sort of way, justify his blasphemous work. Certain elements of the media and members of the literary world in the West have been irresponsible for putting Rushdie on such a high pedestal and it is they who should now put him in the appropriate position that sound intellect demands.

It is in no way being suggested that Rushdie should be handed over to Iran, or any other Muslim country for that matter, or that Rushdie should be put to death : this would go against the very teaching of true Islam as I have explained before.

The way to deal with Rushdie, and this applies to both the Western media and the fundamentalist Muslims, is simply now to forget him. If there is anything that would shock and hurt Rushdie more than what the mullahs have done, it would be the media turning against him and his affair becoming 'domesticated'. He has already expressed his hurt at the 'ugly attitude of the tabloid papers' which pains him most. They routinely trivialise his situation and sneer at him. Can Salman Rushdie, the self-appointed voice of the freedom of speech, deny the tabloid press their right of freedom to express whatever views they wish to? Rushdie's grave concern at being hurt by the tabloid press, often regarded as the 'gutter' press, clearly shows him to belong to the same fraternity. In reality one is hurt the most when the members of one's own close family turn against one. And this certainly is the case with Rushdie and his family of the tabloid press.

Another aspect of the affair that hurts Rushdie is that of being regarded as 'normal'. This goes against his proven chronicle of self-glorification and fame at any cost. To quote the central character from his latest novel : 'How quickly the human mind normalises the abnormal.' (*The Moor's Last Sigh*).

And this can certainly be true of what has happened around Rushdie. He says himself:

'My situation, which would a very short time ago have been considered unthinkable, has become thinkable. Everybody has domesticated it, so now it's usual to make silly jokes about it.'
(Waterstone's Magazine, 1995).

Even if the fatwa were lifted, Rushdie's life would be far from normal. Things have changed for ever for him and this has been hard for him to grasp. He realises himself that 'even if they (mullahs) pledged not to send a hit squad after me, someone could take a pot shot at any time.' (The Times Magazine, 26 August 1995).

There are not too many alternatives left for Rushdie. He has been the author of his own destiny and there are now very few people who feel any sympathy for him. Some of his fervent supporters have become tired of his egotistical motives and of his continual arrogance. It is for his own good that he should become a 'forgotten' man; the more Rushdie becomes a symbol, the more dangerous it is for him. Symbols are invulnerable; they do not need rescuing. There is a risk of a living extinction as his fate becomes the norm in the world's eyes.

Salman Rushdie has for too long been hiding behind his pen, living in a world of make-believe and fiction, aspiring to spread the message of his benefactors. It is about time he woke up into the real world where real people live and where there has to be self-restraint to ensure that the sensitivities and susceptibilities of others are not offended. It is about time he learnt that freedom of expression, like all freedoms, carries its own responsibilities and conditions. Of course, Rushdie has the right to write a book challenging aspects of the Islamic faith, or any faith for that matter. But as someone aware of the deep feelings of Muslims, he must have known that the way he chose to carry out this challenge was bound to provoke fury. This has shown the writer to be gravely irresponsible.

He has also fuelled the fires of anti-Muslim sentiment in the West. It seems that he was deliberately coerced by powers in the West to rouse racial hatred between Muslims and Christians. Rushdie was an opportunist who displayed mercenary qualities which were exploited to the full by powers which will always remain obscure but whose identity is discernible to the astute. Rushdie has been left in the lurch and there is nothing he can do about it. This is no more than he deserves for putting race relations and East/West relations back almost a century.

Like the amateur floor painter Salman Rushdie has written himself into a corner, and there seems to be no way out for the most infamous writer of the century!

161

THE FUTURE

Ever since the mass migration to the western countries of people from Asia, Africa and the Caribbean in the late 1960's, there has been great upheaval in the lives of both the immigrants and the natives whose lands had been 'invaded'. Most of the immigrants were familiar with the Western way of life as their countries had been subjected to imperialist and colonial rule. But for the majority of the West the influx of so many diverse cultures and faiths was too much to handle at one go. Without going too much in depth on this subject, it can be safely accepted that there was a lot of tension and that racism reared its ugly head.

It has also to be said that over a period of time, after hard work by parties from both sides, a 'tolerance zone' had been created in which people were beginning to live together in some sort of harmony, appreciating and respecting each others' cultures and beliefs. Most of the people had begun to realise that the Western world, especially, had become a haven for a multi-cultural and multi-racial society, and that in the safe interests of all concerned, it was better to live in harmony, acknowledging each other's differences, rather than by forcing the ethnic minorities to behave totally like their 'hosts'.

Even despite the fact that Muslims provided the biggest challenge to the West, in that they would not compromise their faith, there was still a great deal of dialogue to try and ensure compatibility. The Pope, too, in a much broader, global manner had stretched his hand in friendship to Islam and there was certainly an air of expectancy.

But, sadly, and almost unforgivably, all this has been undone in a single swoop by Salman Rushdie and whoever else is responsible for the piece of work that has set race relations and religious tolerance back almost a century.

Rather than lauding him with praise and awards Rushdie should be 'tarred and feathered', for all to see what he really is - a vindictive, deceitful, dangerous, unscrupulous mercenary, who has wilfully re-ignited the latent fires of anti-Islamic feeling in the West.

The pieces must be picked up quickly to get back on the right track once again. Happily, there are still a lot of influential people in the West who are judicious and compassionate enough to do exactly that by taking every opportunity to try and create a mutual pact of peace and understanding between Muslims and the West.

A step in the right direction was taken by Prince Charles, the Prince of Wales when he gave a speech at the Oxford Centre for Islamic Studies on 27 October 1993 which won him widespread admiration across the Arab world. This was of great symbolic importance as Prince Charles is heir to the British throne and so, consequently, will be the Defender of the Faith of Britain. He was brave enough to venture into areas which could easily make him unpopular in the eyes of the majority of the indigenous population who have scant regard for their own faith, let alone the 'alien' faith of another people. This step seems an even more courageous one when you add to it the Prince's own personal problems that have diverted the affections of the population more towards his glamorous wife.

TOLERANCE IS A TWO-WAY STREET

Prince Charles called for respect between the two great cultures of Islam and the West, who he said could 'join forces for the sake of our common humanity.' In his speech he also commended British Muslims whom he considers as 'an asset to Britain' because of their 'contribution' to Britain's 'economic well-being and ... cultural richness.'

Prince Charles was also right in pointing out that 'tolerance and understanding must be two-way'. He goes on to clarify the roles of both communities:

'For those of us who are not Muslims, this may mean respect for the daily practice of the Islamic faith and a decent care to avoid actions which are likely to cause deep offence. For the Muslims in our society, there is the need to respect the history, culture and way of life of our country, and to balance their vital liberty to be themselves with an appreciation of the importance of integration.'

(The Times, 28 October 1993).

Whereas most people, Muslims and non-Muslims alike, saw this as a positive way forward, this seemed to have an adverse affect on Rushdie who wrote to The Times in a letter dated 4 November 1993 and published on 8 November where he disapproved of Prince Charles' warning against 'giving offence' to people of different faiths. Rushdie was still playing the same old tune wishing that the whole world would revolve around him.

Gladly Prince Charles remained positive and undeterred, and true to his word he continued the theme of reconciling the two great faiths of the world. He echoed his Oxford speech on a visit to Egypt in March 1995 in which he said that 'the West had formed a mistaken view of the Islamic world.' In an interview with Al-Ahram, he questioned the notion of a clash of civilisations between Islam and the West, and came up with a very perceptive theory that 'what binds our two worlds together is much more powerful than what divides us.' He further elaborates on how the dissensions had been created and how to rectify them:

'Misunderstandings easily arise when we fail to understand how others look at the world and our respective roles in it. In the West, our judgement of Islam has been distorted by taking the extreme as the norm. That is a serious mistake when looking

164

at the Islamic world or at the West.'

(The Daily Telegraph, 13 March 1995).

Surely, this is the way forward. The western media should show Islam in a clear and positive light in the way that Prince Charles continues to do so. In a conference held in London in March 1995 on Britain's role in the world, Prince Charles extended his admiration for Islam by urging Britain 'to learn from Islam and appreciate some of its spiritual tenets to create a unique international role as the 'bridge-builder' between the Muslim world and the West.'

Prince Charles is also aware that this could not be possible unless Britain learns to respect spiritual matters:

'This could not be done without a willingness on our part to learn from the world of Islam and to balance our innate pragmatism with an acute awareness of the vital importance of the things of the Spirit.'

(The Daily Telegraph, 30 March 1995).

Prince Charles delivered the '*coup-de-grace*' to those that are intent on keeping the divide between Islam and the West in Jonathan Dimbleby's documentary (shown on British television in 1994), in which Prince Charles said he would like to be seen as a 'Defender of Faith' - Muslim as well as Christian!

Suggestions and advice for bridging the gap between Islam and the West seem to be coming from all corners. It is hoped that these views are highlighted more in the media so that positive steps can be taken rather than sensationalising the actions of a handful of fundamentalists or extremists who are to be found in all faiths and civilisations.

Noel Malcolm of The Daily Telegraph reacted strongly to an 'extraordinary announcement' by Willie Claes, the new Nato Secretary-General, 'that Islam had replaced Communism as the main threat to Nato.' Malcolm is well aware of the pre-conceived ideas in the West about Islam that have led to this damaging statement as

165

he writes:

> 'the biggest problem is a failure of understanding by politicians and other opinion-makers in the West, who believe that Islam is a monolithic and alien thing, otherwise known as 'fundamentalism', which threatens us all.'

Malcolm advises the British politicians to follow the example of Prince Charles and in referring to his visit to Egypt in March 1995 he picks out the most significant part of that visit:

> 'This visit was also devoted to one special task that the Prince is making more and more his own: building bridges between this country and the world of Islam. It is strange that our politicians seem so much less interested in this task than the man who is going to become Supreme Governor of the Church of England.'

> (The Daily Telegraph, 16 March 1995).

Articles of this nature do leave a positive imprint on the mind of free-thinking readers. For example, in direct response to Noel Malcolm's comments, Simon Cooke, a Conservative Party member from Bradford, West Yorkshire wrote a letter to the editor in which he welcomed Malcolm's remarks and added his condemnation of racism within his political party. Though the letter is partly a clarion-call for his party, the overriding theme is of tolerance and understanding. Mr. Cooke urges that his 'party's leaders must condemn... racism and if necessary expel those who hold such views.' Mr. Cooke renews Prince Charles' reasonings on working on the similarities of the different cultures rather than on the differences:

> 'Most Muslims share the same concerns as the rest of us - poor education, family breakdown, rising levels of crime and violence and wasteful government. To gain support Conservatives should hold back from condemning Islam on the basis of a few extremists.'

> (The Daily Telegraph, 21 March 1995).

Another avenue of bridging the gap has been explored by the Right Reverend Michael Nazir Ali, Britain's first Asian Diocesan Bishop. Perhaps he has modified his views and has now called for the Holy Qur'an to be studied by the West which 'would lead to an historical awareness of Islam,' and 'should lead also to an interest in the literary background to the Koran.' In his latest book, *Mission and Dialogue* (published 30 March 1995), he also exhorts Muslims and their theologians to rise to the challenge of modernity. Dr. Ali seems to be aware that 'international society needs a dialogue of reconciliation today between Western and Islamic thinkers' and that 'such a development, if it were to promote a better understanding between Muslim and Christian societies, would enhance the spirit and temper of Islam itself as well as act as a force for global good.' (The Times, 30 March 1995).

If this is to be the true motive for the study of the Qu'ran, then the idea should be welcomed and applauded, but if the Qur'an is to be subjected to critical study in order to distort its meaning and message, then this will prove no different than the previous superficial attempts to bridge the gap between Islam and the West that date back to the Middle Ages. The true motives of at least one of the theologians of the 16th century, Luther, have been clearly exposed by Hans Kung:

'For his part, Luther had spoken out in favor of translating and publishing the Qu'ran, but only so that everyone could see what an accursed, shameful, desperate book it was, full of lies, fabrications, and all sorts of horrors.'

(Christianity and the World Religions, p. 20).

Let us hope that these 'sorts of horrors' are never inflicted on anyone ever again and that true 'freedom of speech and expression' is granted to those that are striving to bridge the divide for a peaceful and tolerant world.

Who knows, if the true picture and message of Islam is allowed to be manifested justly, then maybe, just maybe, the vision of Noel Malcolm, which he enthused about in The Daily Telegraph of 16

167

March 1995, will not sound so flippant and so wildly fanciful as it may do now when he talks about the Premiership of Britain:

'Perhaps Mr. Major, who is desperate for new ideas about how to win the next election, should do what credulous Muslims think the Prince (Charles) has done already, and convert to Islam. Tories pride themselves on having had the first Jewish Prime Minister. Is this not the logical next step?'

It should be realised that only true Islam paves the way for universal peace and harmony. And for that end both Islam and the West have to be allowed to develop towards that goal without any prejudices or past preconceptions. The renowned Islamic scholar Wilfred Cantwell Smith observed as far back as 1956 that a healthy and functioning Islam was crucial because it had helped Muslim people to cultivate decent values and ideals which are also shared in the West because they spring from a common tradition. He also points out the 'fundamental weakness' of both Western civilisation and Christianity in the modern world which:

'is their inability to recognise that they share the planet not with inferiors but with equals. Unless Western civilisation intellectually and socially, politically and economically, and the Christian church theologically, can learn to treat other men with fundamental respect, these two in their turn will have failed to come to terms with the actualities of the twentieth century.'

(*Islam and Modern History*, p. 305).

Karen Armstrong also supports this view in her book *Muhammad, A Western Attempt To Understand Islam*:

'We in the West have never been able to cope with Islam: our ideas of it have been crude and dismissive and today we seem to believe our own avowed commitment to tolerance and compassion by our contempt for the pain and inchoate distress in the Muslim world. ... Islam is not going to disappear or wither away; it would have been better if it had remained healthy and strong. We can only hope that it is not too late.'

168

She is also forthcoming in the way forward for both communities:

'The reality is that Islam and the West share a common tradition. From the time of the Prophet Muhammad, Muslims have recognised this, but the West cannot accept it..... The beloved figure of the Prophet Muhammad became central to one of the latest clashes between Islam and the West during the Salman Rushdie affair. If Muslims need to understand our Western traditions and institutions more thoroughly today, we in the West need to divest ourselves of some of our prejudice. Perhaps one place to start is with the figure of Muhammad: a complex, passionate man who sometimes did things that it is difficult for us to accept, but who had genius of a profound order and founded a religion and a cultural tradition that was not based on the sword - despite the Western myth - and whose name 'Islam' signifies peace and reconciliation.'

(pp. 265/266).

EPILOGUE

Rushdie: Haunted by His Unholy Ghosts has been an attempt to defend Islam and its noble personalities, especially the Holy Prophet Muhammad(sa), while also trying to expose those who have been guilty of playing the 'fiction' card and causing offence to millions and millions of its adherents. It is the right of any law-abiding citizen of any country to demand that justice be served and also to assist in exposing the names of those who are guilty of any offence.

We do not demand that the likes of Rushdie and their accomplices be put to the guillotine; we would simply like their mischief to be exposed to the world so that in future no one is allowed to inflict such wilful hurt on the adherents of any faith, and not just those of Islam.

I hope that the readers will have been able to judge for themselves as to the truth behind the whole episode, the most distressing aspect of which has been the untold damage it has caused to the name of Islam. Religion should always be judged from the sources upon which it is based, and not from the actions and pronouncements of a handful of fanatics or politicians.

The Islam taught and practised by the Holy Prophet(sa) is a most beautiful and attractive religion, without any blemishes. It is this Islam which will captivate the hearts of the entire world if it is given a chance to flourish. We can only hope and pray that the whole world becomes more tolerant and that it exercises more control over the 'freedoms' it professes to give everyone, and that as the very name of Islam suggests, we can all live in Peace for always. Amen!

170

APPENDICES

APPENDIX A

RUSHDIE'S STATEMENTS

The following quotes show the progression of Rushdie's statements
to the press as the saga around his book developed.

February 1989

'If you don't want to read a book, you don't have to read it. It's
very hard to be offended by *The Satanic verses*.'

'(*Satanic Verses*) was not an attack on Islam or any other religion.'

'Almost everything in those sections - the dream sequences -
starts from an historical or quasi-historical basis.'

'Frankly, I wish I'd written a more critical book ... it seems that
Islamic fundamentalism could do with a little criticism right now.'

'As author of *The Satanic Verses*, I recognise that Muslims in
many parts of the world are genuinely distressed by the publication
of my novel ... we must all be conscious of the sensibilities of others.'

December 1990

'Although I came from a Muslim family background, I was never
brought up as a believer ... But I am able now to say that I am a
Muslim.'

172

'I will continue to work for a better understanding of Islam in the world, as I have always attempted in the past.'

February 1992

'Offence is not, and must never be, a reason for censorship in a free society.'

'I wish that the (British) Government would make it a little easier for me to believe that they're strongly and resolutely on my side.'

August 1995

'*Satanic Verses*' is a serious novel, a moral novel ... It is neither filthy nor degrading nor abusive ... It is a work of art.'

September / October 1995

'We will not allow priests to tell us when we have to shut up ... stirring things up is our proper function in any society.'

'If you do not take risks, you can't do anything interesting.'

APPENDIX B

GLOSSARY

Abdulla bin Ubayy
Leader of the Khazraj tribe of Medina and expected to be crowned king of the City before the arrival of the Holy Prophet(sa). Also known as the leader of the hypocrites.

Ahmadi
A member of the Ahmadiyya Sect.

Ahmadiyya Sect
A Muslim sect which believes Hadhrat Mizra Ghulam Ahmad(as) to be the promised Messiah.

Aisha
Daughter of Hadhrat Abu Bakr and wife of the Holy Prophet(sa).

Allah
The personal and proper name of the Almighty God in Arabic according to Muslims.

Ansars (Helpers)
Muslim residents of Medina at the time of the migration of the Holy Prophet(sa). Each of them was paired with a refugee (Emigrant) from Mecca so they could look after each other better.

Aryas
A militant Hindu sect.

Ayatollah Khomeni	Religious Iranian leader whose original name was Ruholla Moussavi. He became a chief political figure in 1979 after the overthrow of the Shah.
Azraeel	Angel of Death
Banu Quraiza	A Jewish tribe extant in Medina when the Holy Prophet(sa) migrated there.
Bilal	A freed slave who became Islam's first muezzin.
Burqa (veil)	Garment commonly used by Muslim ladies to cover themselves from head to toe when going out.
Companions of the Holy Prophet	Those people who affirmed the truth of the Holy Prophet(sa) during his lifetime and were a witness to his actions.
Djinn	Such beings that remain hidden or aloof from the common people. According to popular myth, these beings have supernatural powers and are synonymous with the Western Concept of the Genie.
Emigrants	Muslim refugees mainly from Mecca who arrived in Medina at the time of the Holy Prophet's migration there.
Eid-ul-Fitr	Muslim festival celebrated at the end of the month of fasting.
Farishta	Angel.
Fatwa	A religious edict.
Faust	A magician and alchemist in German legend who sold his soul to the Devil in exchange for power and worldly experience.

175

Gibreel	Character associated with the Angel Gabriel (Gibreel in Urdu) who was responsible for the transmission of the revelations to the Holy Prophet(sa).
Hadhrat Muhammad(sa)	The Holy Prophet of Islam
Hadith	The traditions of the Holy Prophet(sa).
Halal	That which is lawful under rules of Islam.
Hamza	Uncle of the Holy Prophet(sa) who accepted Islam and was killed at the battle of Uhud.
Hijab	The name given in *The Satanic Verses* to the alleged brothel that is said to have existed in Mecca.
Hindus	Adherents of the Hindu faith, mainly found in India.
Holy Qur'an	The Holy book of the Muslims comprising word for word the revelations of Allah to Muhammad(sa).
Houris	Commonly used to describe chaste and pure companions in the afterlife for the virtuous. The language is strictly figurative and not literal.
Islam	A word literally meaning peace or submission to the will of Allah. According to Muslims it is the name given by Allah to their religion.
Jahliyya	Period of ignorance before advent of the Holy Prophet(sa).
Jihad	A Holy War not necessitating military conflict. It can include a struggle against satanic teachings or designs and against evil within oneself.

Ka'aba	The first house of worship ever built in this world. It is situated in Mecca, Arabia and all Muslims face towards it during their prayers.
Kahin	Soothsayer.
Khadija	The first wife of the Holy Prophet(sa).
Khalid bin Waleed	The greatest military general of early Islam.
Khalifa	A religious successor or a prophet of God.
Lat	Goddess whose idol was housed in a rich temple at Taif.
Mahdi	A word literally meaning "one who is rightly guided." The Holy Prophet(sa) prophesied his advent in the latter days to revive Islam.
Mahound	Derogatory name given to the Holy Prophet Muhammad(sa) by Western Orientalists; historically a demonic figure, or bogeyman.
Manat	Goddess whose temple was at Qudayd on the Red Sea.
Martin Luther	Leader of the Reformation in Germany and founder of the Lutheran Church in the 16th Century.
Mecca	A city in Arabia where the Holy Prophet(sa) was born and where the Ka'aba is situated.
Medina	A city in Arabia formerly known as Yahthrib. It is about 424km north of Mecca, and is the place where the Holy Prophet(sa) migrated when he was forced to flee Mecca.
Mephistopheles	The name of the evil spirit to whom Faust was said to have sold his soul.

Mount Hira	Located about 3 miles from Mecca. It was in a cave on this mountain that the Holy Prophet(sa) used to retire for meditation and where he received his first revelation.
Mount Sinai	Located somewhere in the mountain district of the Sinai peninsula and where Moses(as) received the ten commandments.
Muezzin	A person who calls out the Adhan (call to prayer).
Mughals	The ruling dynasty of Kings in India before the advent of British Rule there.
Mullah	A Muslim religious priest.
Partition	Commonly used to describe the events in 1947 when British India was partitioned into Pakistan and India, after independence from colonial rule.
Promised Messiah	A reformer whose advent has been prophesied by both Jesus(as) and the Holy Prophet(sa), who was to revive religion. The term is commonly used for Hadhrat Mizra Ghulam Ahmad(as) of Qadian, who claimed to be such a reformer.
Purdah	Essentially involves the seperation of men and women in society. Thus men and women are required to restrain their looks and women are expected to wear an outer garment or Hijab when going out.
Quraish	An Arab tribe to which the Holy Prophet(sa) belonged. They were descendants of Fihr, who was in turn a descendant of Ishmael and Abraham (May Allah be pleased with them).
Safwan	A servant of Aisha.

Sahih Bukhari	The foremost of the six most authentic books of traditions of the Holy Prophet(sa). It was compiled by Imam Bukhari.
Saladin	A Muslim sultan of Syria and Egypt from 1169. He was the principle adversary of the Crusades and the conqueror of Jerusalem for the Muslims. Much admired for his qualities of chivalry, intelligence and compassion.
Salman Farsi	A companion of the Holy Prophet(sa) who originated from the land of Fars or Persia.
Shaitan	Satan.
Sharia	Islamic Law.
Sufis	Muslim mystics originating from the 11th Century.
Surat	A chapter of the Holy Qur'an.
Tirmidhi	One of the six most authentic books of Hadith, or traditions of the Holy Prophet(sa).
Tabari	References taken from the chronicle of the Prophet's campaigns by Muhammad ibn Umar-al-Waqidi.
Talmud	Collection of Jewish religious and civil laws, together with scholarly interpretations of their meanings. Ranks second to the Bible as the most sacred and influential work of the Jewish religion.
Ulama (Ulema)	Muslim religious scholars.
Umar (2nd Caliph)	The second successor to the Holy Prophet(sa).
Uzza	Goddess whose shrine was located in the valley of Nakhla near Mecca.

Zayd Bin Harith	Freed slave of the Holy Prophet(sa) and his adopted son.
Zaynab Bint Haritha	Divorced wife of Zaid bin Harith and later married to the Holy Prophet(sa).
Zia-ul-Haq	President of Pakistan from 1977 to 1988.
Zulfikhar Ali Bhutto	President of Pakistan from 1971 to 1977.
Zurqani	Sharh Zurqani, by Mohammad ibn 'Abd al-Baqi al-Zurqani, an Islamic Historian.

REFERENCES

Victory of Islam, Hadhrat Mizra Ghulam Ahmad, 1890 English edition, Tameerr Press, Lahore, Pakistan 1973.

Muhammad: Seal of the Prophets, Muhammad Zafrulla Khan, Routledge & Kegan Paul, London 1980.

Christianity and the World Religions, Hans Kung, William Collins & Co Ltd, London 1987.

The Rise of Christian Europe, Hugh Trevor-Roper, Thames & Hudson, London 1965.

Treason Against God, Leonard W. Levy, Schocken Books, London 1981.

Mohammed, Maxime Rodinson, 1961 English edn., Allen Lane, The Penguin Press, London 1971.

Islam: A Christian Perspective, Michael Nazir-Ali, The Paternoster Press, Exeter 1983.

Muslim-Christian Encounters, William Montgomery Watt, Routledge, London 1991.

Islamic Fundamentalism and Modernity, Professor W.M. Watt, Routledge, London 1988.

Muhammad at Medina, W. Montgomery Watt, The Clarendon Press, Oxford 1956.

Islam and the West, Norman Daniel, The University Press, Edinburgh 1958.

Muhammad: A Western Attempt to Understand Islam, Karen Armstrong, Victor Gollancz Ltd, London 1991.

The Satanic Verses, Salman Rushdie, Viking Penguiin 1988

Grimus, Salman Rushdie, Victor Gollancz Ltd, London 1975

Midnight's Children, Salman Rushdie, Jonathan Cape Ltd, London 1983.

Shame, Salman Rushdie, Jonathan Cape Ltd, London 1983.

Haroun and the Sea Stories, Salman Rushdie, Granta Books, London 1990.

East, West, Salman Rushdie, Jonathan Cape Ltd, London 1994.

The Waterstone's Magazine, a quarterly magazine published by Waterstone's Booksellers, UK.

Muhammad, Martin Lings, George Allen & Unwin, London 1983.

Transforming Light, Albert & E. Vail, Jasper & Row 1970.

World's History, Rodney Castleden, Parragon 1994.

The Moors in Spain, Stanley Lane-Poole, Darf Publishers Ltd, London 1984

Structure of Spanish History, Americo Castro (p.170)

A History of the Crusades, Sir Steven Runciman, Harmondsworth, Penguin 1965.

La Guerre et le Gouvernement de L'Algerie, M Baudricourt, Paris, 1853.

Polemique Byzantine Contre L'Islam, Adel-Theodore Khoury, Leiden: Brill 1972

Love and Living, Thomas Merton, Bantam Books, New York 1980.

The Spirit of Islam, Ameer Ali Syed, 1873.

Modern Trends in Islam, Sir Hamilton Gibb, University of Chicago Press, 1947.

An Interpretation of Islam, Professor Laura Veccia Vaglieri

De Religione Mohammedica, Adrian Reland, 1705.

The Talmud Unmasked, Rev. I.B. Pranaitis.

Ash Wednesday Supper, Giordano Bruno 1584, English edition, William Boulting, 1914.

Islam and Modern History, William Cantwell Smith, 1956.

NEWSPAPERS

The Times	Published in the UK
The Sunday Times	Published in the UK
The Times Magazine	Published in the UK
The Independent	Published in the UK
The Independent on Sunday	Published in the UK
The Guardian	Published in the UK
The Daily Telegraph	Published in the UK
The Washington Times	Published in the USA
The New York Times	Published in the USA

BRITISH TELEVISION STATIONS

BBC2	British Broadcasting Corporation
ITV	Independent Television
CHANNEL 4	Part of ITV